OUTSIDE THE BOX

An American Journey

David H.W. Griswold

OUTSIDE THE BOX An American Journey
Copyright 2020 by David H.W. Griswold

All rights reserved. No part of this book may be used or reproduced by any means, graphic, electronic, or mechanical, including photocopying, recording, taping, or by any information storage retrieval system without written permission of the publisher except in the case of brief quotations embodied in critical articles and reviews.

Cover by Eric D. Griswold

ISBN: 978-1-7344990-5-6

ACKNOWLEDGEMENTS

Special thanks to the author and fellow Marine, Ken McAdams. Without his guidance, literary skills, and encouragement, this book would not have been possible.

Also, to Wick Griswold, and Lynn Patarini, two authors who are responsible for editing and formatting the manuscript into acceptable standards. Their talents, patience, and understanding have been essential to publication.

Dedicated to my mother, Rosalie Wood Griswold, who taught me to be respectful of others, especially those who had different viewpoints, and who instilled in me a love of life that has made this a most enjoyable journey.

TABLE OF CONTENTS

I   **The Beginning**

        Family
        Early Years
        Traditions
        Education
        C. Lambert Heyniger
        My Dad
        Prep School
        My First Car
        College Years
        Motivation
        Induction

II   **Summertime**

        Preparation

III   **Officer Candidate School**

        Staff Sergeant Vic
        Drilling
        The Rifle Range
        Pugil Sticks
        Bernie's Boys
        Weeding Out
        The House Mouse
        Basic School

IV   Gearing Up

        Camp Lejeune
        Massacre on the Boardwalk
        30 Days Off
        Flight to Combat
        Okinawa

V   Welcome to the Nam

        Assignments
        Staff Sergeant Ron
        Lieutenant Barry
        Troops
        Convoys
        Stand Off at The Bridge
        Helicopter Fire
        Patrols
        To Fire or Not to Fire
        China Beach
        A Strong Arm
        Embarkation School
        The Tet Offensive
        Graves Registration
        Guarding the Perimeter
        Transitions
        Captain Bob
        Ambushed
        R&R
        Company Commander
        New Officer
        Farewell to the Nam

VI	**Welcome Home**

        Arrivals
        Parties

VII	**Adjusting to the States**

        California Duty
        Marriage
        Coaching
        Ira Hayes
        The Reserves
        Baseball and Raisins
        Boat Trip
        Jobs
        The Painting Company
        Career Consulting
        Elaine

VIII	**Conclusion**

        Reflections

FOREWARD

My life was prescribed by an aristocratic family that resided in a large family compound in a beautiful part of Connecticut. I would go to the prescribed prep schools, prescribed colleges, join the prescribed clubs, marry the prescribed woman, and work for the prescribed company. If I went into the service, it was the sixties, and the draft was in full swing, it would have been the prescribed service.

My career path was laid out very nicely. All I had to do was check off the boxes at the assigned times, and a special version of the American Dream would be mine to savor. I failed to check off any one of them. It was not rebellion. I wanted to follow the prescribed plan-it just didn't work out.

As a result, I was looked at with concern if not disdain by the family. I did not fit in.

I graduated from lesser-known schools and enlisted in the last service my family would have selected, the Marines! Plugged into America's most controversial war-Vietnam, I relied on the wisdom and instincts of men my family would never have acknowledged. It was 180 degrees from the family blueprint for success. After Vietnam, I went from the most prestigious clubs in New York City to the highly competitive athletics fields of Florida and Alabama. Along the way, I met an interesting cast of characters that helped shape my life in so many ways. Many of them were such a deviation from the prescribed plan; it was nothing short of hilarious. Other experiences were sad and challenging as I struggled to meet my families' expectations.

Of all my adventures, there is no question that my military career was the most poignant and had the most impact on my life. All the stories and events described here are true to the best of my recollection; it was over fifty years ago. I did change some of the sequences of events for the sake of continuity. Some of the names are accurate; other names have been changed to spare embarrassment, sadness, or perhaps lawsuits. Further, a few of the characters represent composites of people, and any identification with any one individual would be inaccurate.

Finally, the events and the emotions surrounding them are mine and mine alone. My stories are narrated through my eyes without collaboration from anyone. Many stories brought back smiles and laughs and were easy to write. Other events were buried deeper in my mind and brought back tears as I recalled them.

Outside the Box is a journey that describes the challenges, perils, frustrations, and fun experienced by deviating from the expected. If the narrative appears to be a roller coaster of emotions, it is because it was.

Thank you for your indulgence.
DHWG

The Beginning

The engines of the military transport plane droned on as we headed southwest from the island of Okinawa. It was a full flight, but no one spoke. Everyone was lost in their thoughts. My thoughts centered on, would I succeed? Would I be able to command troops? Would I meet the high expectations? Would I be wounded? Would I die? And even more important to me at the time, would I regain the acceptance of my family. Would I be considered a promising member or a misfit? I was both confident and unsure. It was back and forth a mixture of emotions.

I was jarred from these thoughts as the pilot's voice came over the intercom. "We are approaching our destination. We will come in fast and hard. Once we land get off in a hurry, we do not stay long on the runway."

No sooner had that message been received than the plane plunged into a rapid descent. Since I am not comfortable in a plane, to begin with, this was a terrifying maneuver. Then the plane banked sharply to the left.

From my window, you saw the dark waters of the South China Sea. From the other side, you could make out mountains silhouetted against the skyline. The plane leveled off, and we could see the runway. As the pilot said, we came in fast and landed hard. The engines reversed, and we were thrown back in our seats. No sooner had the plane stopped than the ramp at the rear opened, and we rapidly exited. A blast of hot, humid air hit us. It was September, but the humidity was stifling. Adjusting to the heat, we were directed to a building and quickly herded inside. Looking back over my shoulder, I noticed our plane was gone.

We were processed and jogged back across the runway to tents full of cots.

"Sleep here, you will be assigned in the morning," said a voice from the rear of the tent. "Oh, and welcome to Danang, Vietnam."

How did this happen? It was 1967, and the Vietnam war was in full swing. Danang was a port city, home to the First Marine Division. The center of activity revolved around the giant airbase in Danang. From here, Marine Corps fighter jets flew countless missions in support of all Marine operations. They also flew into North Vietnam to contain the flow of supplies headed south into South Vietnam along the Ho Chi Min trail.

How had I arrived here at age 23? My life had been planned out by my family, and all I had to do was follow the plan. This was definitely not in the plan.

Family

Born in the early forties, my life path was planned out by the family elders. My parents were in full agreement, and they would implement a program for their son that had worked for generations. As a result, my parents had a strong and lasting influence. They would guide me to follow the prescribed plan.

My Father

My Dad grew up in Erie, Pennsylvania. His grandfather had moved his immediate family from Connecticut to Erie, Pennsylvania, and founded the Griswold Manufacturing Company. They made cast iron skillets, which today are collectors' items. His father became president of the company, and my Dad and his two brothers all worked at various times in the frying pan business.

Dad was the middle of three boys. His older and younger brothers were different. Both were extremely smart, driven, and successful. The oldest would graduate from Yale and serve the University on their medical staff. Later, he would practice medicine in the town of Old Lyme and form clinics to combat diseases. Towards the end of his life, he would serve as a community leader and be responsible for leading committees that maintained the beauty and charm of our town. His vision would be appreciated, and he was highly respected both in medicine and for community projects. The youngest graduated from Yale, majoring in engineering with an emphasis on aeronautical design. He built a wind tunnel behind his garage and would study the flight of aircraft. This study would help with the design and flight of gliders that were used in the Normandy invasion. Later, he was a driving force in bringing the safety harness used in a seatbelt to the automotive industry. His knowledge of engineering principles and aviation flight was acknowledged and respected. Into his eighties, he was requested to consult with NASA, Sikorsky, and Northrop Grumman along with other aviation corporations. Both uncles were friendly to me but very serious. They set high expectations for their nephew. I liked them and respected their positions but was intimidated by their personalities and success.

Dad was far more easy-going. He had a pleasant personality and made friends easily. Dad was good looking and coupled with charm, he could be the life of the party. People were drawn to him and enjoyed his company. He was comfortable and fun to be around.

At 6'2' and 195 lbs., Dad was an exceptionally good athlete. He had the perfect build for sports. His sport was tennis. A champion of Western Pennsylvania, he played against the two greatest players of the times-Don Budge and Bill Tilden. In today's world, he could have made a handsome living playing tennis. But in those days, it was simply exhibitions and a collection of silver trays, plates, and cups.

I admired him for many reasons. First, I loved his personality, which was to take life as it came and enjoy the people around you. Second, I idolized his athletic ability. I envied all his trophies and silver plates and thought that I, too, would someday be recognized for sports accomplishments. But even more important, I wanted to be popular and have the attention and adoration that came so easily to him. There is no question that he influenced me and affected my early development.

Dad married early in life and had two small children when the family fortunes took a downward turn during the great depression of '29. As the money disappeared, so did his wife, leaving him with the two children. Frustrated by the ending of his marriage, Dad spent most of his time on the tennis courts. It was there he met my mother at a well-publicized tennis match.

Introduced by a cousin, they fell in love almost immediately and were married shortly after that. It was a fine marriage—a prominent and well-respected family on his side and another prominent family on hers.

What could be better!

As my parents settled into their home, the Griswold Manufacturing Company, which had slowly declined, became locked in a family battle over its future. One side had more stock than the other, and the business ultimately sold to a New York firm against the desire of our side of the family. The new owners wasted little time declaring there was no need for the Griswold's. Thus, my father and his two brothers would leave Erie and move back to Connecticut.

For my father, this represented a serious decline in the family fortunes and a challenge for a man with a new wife and a young family.

**My Father
William B Griswold**

My Mother

My mother was born in Pennsylvania, where her father, Harry Wood, had graduated from Princeton and had put his education to good use. He was remarkably successful in the oil business. To be more specific, he owned a company that refined oil for a company that was later to be known as Pennzoil.

Flush with cash, my grandfather Wood decided that refining oil was rather boring. The real money and excitement lay in finding the oil. He wanted to be a wildcatter and make big money. The place he selected for locating the oil was Kentucky. I often wondered what would have happened if his choice had been Texas.

He moved the family to Lexington, Kentucky, and the early years there were grand. My mother and her two brothers frequented the finest clubs and socialized with the Claiborne's, Hancock's, and Whitney's-old Kentucky families that excelled in thoroughbred racing. My mother fitted well in this environment. She became a southern belle and learned social graces at a young age. She could charm anyone, and her love of people and parties made her extremely popular.

She and my father were a perfect match. They loved to entertain, and as a boy, I would watch them preside over multiple parties. They hosted these gatherings with grace and charm, and I watched with pride as people gravitated to these gatherings. They made it look easy, and I wanted to have the same type of life. Both my parents passed their love of the good life on to their only son.

Unfortunately, my grandfather did not find oil in Kentucky. Dry hole after dry hole depleted the family fortunes.

Thus, my parents, who had grown up in comfortable surroundings, now found themselves in the very unfamiliar situation of being essentially broke. Lack of funds, combined with my mother's assessment that Erie, Pennsylvania, was the coldest, most dreary place on earth, pressured my father to follow his brothers and return to the family compound in Connecticut.

When I was two years old, my family moved back to Connecticut. They moved into a rented house on Rogers Lake. The first day there may have been an omen. It was around five o'clock in the afternoon. Mom and Dad were halfway through the unenviable task of unpacking and were enjoying a well-deserved cocktail. Suddenly there was a loud splash in the lake.

"Boy, that was a big bass," said my father "This is going to be great."

"By the way," asked my mother, "Have you seen David?"

"I thought he was with you," replied Dad.

"Oh my God," they exclaimed simultaneously, and both ran out of the house. My athletic father covered the ground quickly, and sure enough, there was his young son floating face down in the lake. Dad jumped in and pulled me out. I was coughing and sputtering. It was October. The lake was cold.

"He is OK, but he is shivering," said my Dad. "What should we do?"

Mother had an all-purpose remedy that covered multiple situations. "Give him a shot of bourbon."

And thus, my first day in Connecticut was off to an auspicious start.

Growing up in Connecticut in the fifties, the reversal of our family fortunes was eased a bit. We had relatives that were well off, so there was always a roof over our heads and enough food and clothes to get by. But it was a strange time. While Mom and Dad were just surviving, my aunts and uncles had escaped our predicament. Through good investments and marrying into money, they enjoyed beautiful homes, expensive cars, and European travel. I was exposed to the good life through my association with them. Still, I was grounded in the sense of reality when Mom and Dad would sit at the kitchen table and try and figure out what bills they could pay. It was an interesting dichotomy.

**My Mother
Rosalie Wood Griswold**

Early years

My early childhood was comfortable and predictable. By now, my family had moved down to the shore. No one locked their homes or their cars, there was very little crime, and no companies were moving out of state. Jobs were plentiful and secure. Everyone worked, and companies paid a fair wage with good benefits. Divorce was unheard of. Families stayed together. Summers were baseball and swimming; winters were ice hockey and sledding. School was very enjoyable. Pleasant women taught motivated and respectful students. Mrs. Carlson taught third grade, Mrs. Muller, fourth, and Mrs. Champion fifth. Grading was easy, and the biggest problem faced by teachers was talking in class and chewing gum. Everyone got along.

What I remember most about growing up was Little League Baseball. While I did not have my father's size, I did have his hand-eye coordination and was able to make the team for three years. Back in the '50s, Little League Baseball was a big deal in our town. There was only one team, and we played the other towns in the area. We liked and respected our opponents with one exception. We hated Saybrook, and they felt the same way about us. To add to the drama, we were the two best teams and always played for the championship. I remember one game in particular. It was played in Saybrook, and the score was one to one after six innings. In the seventh, we scored the winning run on a close play at home plate. The call could have gone either way, but it went to us.

The Saybrook crowd started on to the field to argue with the umpire and, in the process, started yelling at us. I was ten at the time, and being yelled at for winning a game was a little unnerving. With that, the Old Lyme crowd came on the field. These were Machniks, McGoverns, Tookers, Swaneys, and Griffiths. Tough men who worked in construction, trades, and farming. It turned into a full-scale fight, and it was generally agreed, Old Lyme won both the game and the fight. I was caught up in the emotions of the two towns, and it put pressure on me to win and defend the honor of our town.

During my three years of playing, I was fortunate to have three dedicated coaches. Dave Connors, Allen Dean, and Ray Smith. They all knew baseball and were skilled at teaching us the game. This was especially true of Ray Smith. He had played professional baseball in the St. Louis Cardinal organization. We were always asking him to show us how he could hit. He had avoided this request in the past, but on this day, he agreed. Our best pitcher, Ray Kevitt, threw what we considered a very good fastball, and Ray swung. Our field was behind the old center school. The ball sailed over the first building, the courtyard, and hit the roof on the front of the school, traveled into the schoolyard, and rolled into the street in front of the Town Hall. It must have gone at least 400 feet. We had never seen a ball hit that far.

All three coaches were incredibly patient with me and my overwhelming desire to win. It wasn't easy for them. One time I struck out with men on base and took out my frustrations by slamming my fist into the cement dugout wall. That resulted in two broken bones in my hand. Not too smart. The doctor wanted to put it in a cast, but I insisted on having it taped and playing through the season. Another time, I was thrown out of a game for arguing with the umpires. Many coaches would have been worn out with my antics, but all three men worked with me and tried to harness my emotions.

As mentioned, we battled Saybrook, and my last season, we won the championship. I made wonderful friends and enjoyed being part of the teams. My parents were proud. Yet, happy as I was to be part of a winning team, I was bothered that I was not the best player. There were at least three better players on that team. I wanted to be the best. It was strange because no one pushed me. Dad was simply happy I was on the team, and my mother could not understand why I was so competitive. But I was. I took the game as a challenge to be the athlete my father was, and I felt I was falling short. My Dad would pitch and hit balls to me every day, and I would be upset with the slightest mistake. I had to excel. My frustrations and desire to be the best took away some of the enjoyment of the game. My burning desire to achieve and make my family proud would only grow over time.

As I entered my mid-teenage years, I became more aware of my family's background and the intense pressure it would bring to conform and succeed. The Griswold's had founded the town we lived in and were considered a very prestigious family. Mathew Griswold the First had settled on Griswold Point with a land grant from the English government in 1640. Today, Mathew Griswold, the twelfth, resides on the Point making the Griswold's the oldest family in America to reside in a single location continuously.

The Griswold family has gone on to make a mark for themselves as governors, senators, doctors, engineers, lawyers, and successful businessmen. To continue their success, education was stressed, and since the family lived within an hour from New Haven, the college of choice was Yale University. All the Griswold's went to Yale. There was no other school to be considered. Princeton, Columbia, Dartmouth, etc. were no match and Harvard being unthinkable. My great, great grandfather, great grandfather, grandfather, father, his two brothers, and my many cousins, all went to Yale. If you were a Griswold, you followed that tradition. Growing up as the youngest of my generation, I was expected to follow in the family footsteps. I received Yale jackets for Christmas and Yale shirts for summer. We attended Yale sporting events, Yale theater, and Yale museums. Often the family would gather, and as the evenings progressed and the liquor flowed freely, Yale songs would be sung. "March, March on Down the Field," "Good Night Poor Harvard," and "Bulldog, Bulldog, Bow Wow Wow" would echo through the house. By the time they got around to the "Whiff 'n Poof Song"- "We are poor little lambs that have gone astray"-there wasn't a dry eye in the house-nor I might add, a full liquor bottle. It was all great fun, and I couldn't wait to be accepted and wear a smart blue blazer with a large Y over the breast pocket.

Boola, Boola!

Traditions

Along with Yale, other traditions were important and expected. After Yale, I would be employed in a family business or a profession. One uncle was a doctor, another an engineer, and my father owned his own business. What you did was not that important as long as it was professional and made you prosperous. The latter being stressed. Money was never directly discussed as that would be improper, but making the right appearance in the right part of town and connected to the right families was imperative. This blueprint for my success was discussed at our family dinners. Family dinners at my uncles were not just dinners; they were events.

You dressed for dinner. Ties and jackets were mandatory, and most of the gentlemen wore suits with vests, offset with pocket watches. The ladies all wore dresses. I am certain my mother and all my aunts did not own slacks. Arriving at my uncle's home at precisely 6:30, we would be given drinks and canopies in the living room. All my relatives were steeped in the social graces, and the conversation was pleasant and lively. At precisely 7:30 dinner was served in the dining room. The dining room featured a large table that sat twelve. Beautiful silver was laid out on Irish linen, surrounded by fine china. To the right were two Waterford crystal glasses for water and wine. There were name tags, and I found my seat between my parents. The hosting aunt and uncle would be seated at each end, and other relatives filled in the sides. Seating arrangements were important, and they were arranged with the utmost care to ensure you would be seated next to someone who would inspire stimulating conversation. If, by chance, there had been a disagreement during the week, the two contentious parties would be placed at opposite ends to avoid any unpleasantries.

When all were seated, my aunt rang a bell, and two servers appeared with the first course-usually a soup; lobster bisque was a favorite. Another standard was the shrimp cocktail. Everyone looked to my aunt, who was hosting the occasion, and when she picked up her spoon or shrimp fork, it was the signal for all to join in. My aunt had the eye of an eagle, and while making small talk, she watched to be sure everyone was enjoying the first course. As people finished and put down the proper utensil, she rang the bell, and the servers entered, removed the bowl or small dish, and brought in the second course, usually a salad. Walnut and Caesar were the two favorites. After the salads, it would be time to bring in the main course. Warm plates were placed at the head of the table, and the entra was placed on a platter in front of my uncle. Standing rib roast was a favorite. The potatoes were positioned to his right in a silver bowl, and the vegetables set next to my aunt. My uncle carved the meat and then passed the plate to another designated relative who put a generous spoon full of potatoes on the plate and down to my aunt for the vegetables. Sauces and gravy would be passed in silver gravy boats or crystal bowls. They had all done this many times, and the process moved quickly. Then the servers poured the wine. Once all were served, and all the wine poured, everyone looked to the head of the table where my uncle would raise his glass. Good health and good prosperity were sometimes said, but the favorite was "For God, For Country, and For Yale." That would always be met with a "hear, hear," and the meal was consumed.

The main conversation during the meal was centered on politics and business. Eisenhower was President, the

Korean War had ended, and prosperity was growing. This was met with approval. The family was heavily Republican, and everyone liked Ike. Other conversations revolved around travel. All had gone to Europe at one time, or another, and England and France were the most common destinations. Hotels and restaurants were evaluated. Other topics were more local. The family took great interest in the town their ancestors had founded. Keeping the town void of tacky stores and dirty factories was paramount. Local gossip would be discussed but always in polite tones.

One example of how the family addressed local issues was the announcement that a large factory would be built on land near the family homestead. It was a perfect location for a factory adjacent to a rail line and with plenty of water to cool the giant turbines in the plant. There had never been a factory in the town, and while it would provide jobs, it would alter the landscape and the property values.

"Can you imagine a factory with belching smoke and large trucks going in and out day and night" decried my cousin.

"Factories breed factories," said my uncle.

"It must be stopped" was the unanimous decision.

The family agreed.

To stop the factory, family members phoned other like-minded citizens and formed an association to purchase the land. The next question was what to do with the land? There had to be some return on their investment. After some debate, it was agreed that an 18-hole championship golf course would not only enhance the beauty of the area but would provide a financial return over time. With that in mind, the project of building a golf course got underway. Money was raised, and the entire matter concluded within a year. Today the Blackhall

Golf Club is extremely popular and considered one of the finer private courses in eastern Connecticut.

Another hot topic was the realization that the town business district was overcrowded. The mercantile strip was on the historic main street lined with beautiful old elm and maple trees along with colonial homes dating back to the 1700s. The thought of cutting down trees and destroying colonial-era homes to expand parking lots was a night-mare. The family was appalled.

"What we have here represents our past and has historical significance," said one of my cousins.

"Once it's gone, it's gone forever," cried another.

A decision was reached to move the business section to a deserted part of town. One of my uncles headed up the project. An incorporation of business owners formed, and the businesses were all moved. Today, over 70 years later, the old main street is as beautiful as it was in the 1700s. The new shopping center on Halls Road flourishes with easy access and large parking lots to accommodate the growth of the town.

I did not realize it at the time, but I was getting a real lesson in how power is utilized. Unlike organized crime families that got their way through intimidation and fear with no regard for the law or moral values, our family wielded power by forming corporations, consortiums, partnerships, and associations. It raised capital in formats that allowed for new opportunities, profit returns, and, of course, tax advantages—all legal and with the best of intentions that would withstand the passing of time. Looking back, there was excitement to be a part of such power while watching it conducted with such grace and formality.

Along with business matters, Yale would come up in dinner conversations, and all heads would turn to me, the representative of the next generation. When you are at Yale was always the opening line to be followed by subjects to take, sports to play, and which college within Yale such as Saybrook, Calhoun, Timothy Dwight, Pearson, etc. should I attend. Perhaps I would even be admitted to Skull and Bones, the highly selective and secret society within the University. I would take it all in and just smile. It was quite enjoyable not to have to do much thinking, as others were planning my life. The goal of attending one of the most prestigious schools in the country, followed by a senior position in a well-known company leading to wealth was more than fine by me. After dinner, everyone retired to the den where brandy was poured. More talk would ensue, and around 10 PM, people began to say their goodbyes.

During this time, I said little. Children would be seen and not heard. Although I was in my teenage years, I was considered quite young. Mostly, I just took in what was around me and appreciated the fine china, crystal, and silver. I also appreciated the traditions. It was a glorious time, and I really enjoyed myself.

My Uncles

Dr. Matthew Griswold

Roger W. Griswold II

Education

Then something happened that was not foreseen and certainly not in keeping with the career plan laid out at the family dinners. I started bringing home C's and D's from the local high school. I had sailed through grade school based on easy grading standards and my ability to charm teachers. But high school was different. Instead of one teacher, we had different teachers for different subjects, and they were far more impressed with the knowledge and test scores than charm and family status. This was a problem for me.

I struggled with learning. Later I would be diagnosed with a learning issue. I had an extremely hard time processing new information and retaining facts. Of all the subjects, math was my worst. I was fine with basic math, but algebra was foreign. I did not understand any of it. My Dad was exceptional in math, as were his brothers. They could not understand why I was having trouble. For me, it was bad enough in school struggling to answer or solve problems, but at home, I felt like I was letting down the family. That feeling would haunt me for a lifetime.

The poor grades continued, and even with my family's legacy tradition, you did not get into Yale with C's and D's from high school. Alarmed, my family decreed that I must be sent to private school to improve my grades and, of course, get into Yale.

I was very conflicted about this. Yes, I wanted to follow in my family's footsteps. Still, I had spent two years at the local high school and was enjoying the experience. While my grades were terrible, I was on the high school baseball team and really liked my coach. His name was Ralph Kehoe. Coach Kehoe was not only a great athlete, but he had been an Army captain in Korea. His face had marks from the shrapnel he had received during an attack. Coach had won the Silver Star, Bronze Star, and the Purple Heart. He was hard but fair, and he liked me. I was small for my age and not terribly strong, but I had good hand-eye coordination and could field well. I was the starting second baseman. But my greatest strength was my determination. Nobody worked harder, and I truly got the most out of my ability. Coach Kehoe appreciated that effort and would compliment me on my initiative. Receiving praise from a Silver Star recipient meant a great deal.

Since I was not doing well in the classroom, and teachers were giving me barely passing grades, the praise of Coach Kehoe meant everything. Aside from my parents, he was the first person who seemed to understand my intense desire to achieve, and he had a way of motivating me. He would watch me play, and if I got a hit or made a good play in the field, he would smile and say, "Is that the best you can do," with a slight smile.

I would respond with more commitment than ever. I stayed after practice to run extra laps. I would throw balls against a wall for hours to improve my fielding. I swung a weighted bat to improve my hitting. Coach Kehoe appreciated the effort and would tell the upperclassmen they should have my work ethic. At that point, I would run through a wall for that man.

Then one day, he gave me another lesson. We were in a game, and as a sophomore, I was starting on the varsity at second base. Someone hit a routine grounder to me, and I missed it. I couldn't believe it. I was a good fielder, and the ball just went right under my glove. I was crushed to make such an error on such an easy play. I jogged off the field and was hanging my head. Suddenly Coach Kehoe appeared.

He grabbed me by my shirt and yelled, "Don't ever hang your head. You're better than that."

Today, he would be fired for grabbing a student, but it made an impression. I made other mistakes playing sports, but never again did I feel sorry for myself. I just worked harder. Coach Kehoe was a major influence on my life.

Ralph P. Kehoe

Along with baseball, I became more and more interested in the opposite sex. Typical of my baseball career, there were no home runs. Still, I was a consistent singles hitter and picked up many doubles. Getting to second base was most enjoyable.

In high school, I had many good friends. One of my closest friends at the time was Jimmy Falcone. Jimmy was Italian, and he was 16 going on 25. Jimmy was the Fonz from *Happy Days'* fame. He could get the girls. I loved hanging around with him hoping to pick up a castoff. Jimmy liked me for my athletic ability and my connections. He would educate me on the art of seduction. On occasion, Jimmy would invite me to his home for dinner. Dinner at the Falcone's was slightly different from dinner with my family.

Jeans and sport shirts were the dress code. Mrs. Falcone would have a large bowl of pasta in the kitchen, and everyone picked up silverware and filled up their plastic plates. Next, you scooped out some sauce and returned to the table. On the table would be a loaf of bread with a tub of butter next to it. A bowl of salad was passed around along with an assortment of dressings. Everyone grabbed what they needed. Glasses were mismatched. Some were colorful glasses that once held jelly. I think Yogi Bear was represented on two or three. Soda was the popular drink, although some had milk, and others just brought a beer bottle to the table.

The conversation never centered on politics or business. Instead, the main conversation revolved around cars, equipment, and general repairs. What interested me was everyone seemed to have a specialty. One family member was good in carpentry, another with automotive, and another with plumbing. Whatever the skill, they would agree to help the other. Since I could not fix anything and lacked any mechanical skills, I had little to say, but I would nod my head and agree with whatever was discussed.

It was so different. These families were not as well-schooled or steeped in traditions and not as prosperous, but in another way, they were happy, maybe more so. They seemed to get along and helped one another. While they did not have high-profile professional goals for their children, certainly, they had hope for a good life. Get a good high school education, get married, get a job at the local plant, and settle into a comfortable middle-class lifestyle.

I really liked them.

I found myself going back and forth between my upper-class family and the middle to lower classes of my high school friends. I became comfortable in both situations, a trait that would prove valuable in the coming years.

With my high school sports success and my enjoyment of my high school friends, I had very mixed feelings about going off to prep school. But this was the fifties, and my feelings were not discussed. The family had decided I would go to private school, and I went along.

The private school that was selected was Choate in Wallingford, Connecticut. Today it is known as Choate Rosemary Hall having combined with the girls' school of Rosemary Hall. It was then and still is a feeder school for Yale. Many of my older cousins had gone there. My father was confident I would have no problem. So, with my Mom and Dad, I got in the family car, and we drove up to Choate for the interview. The interview would be a preview of many to come. The headmaster of the school had a resemblance to Mr. Bumble in *Oliver Twist*. A large man with a deep voice, he boomed out,

"So, you want to come to Choate?"

Thoughts of Coach Kehoe, Jimmy Falcone, and high school girls were running through my mind. I said, "Yes," with absolutely no enthusiasm. A fact I am sure was not lost on Mr. Bumble.

"Ah-hem," he muttered. "Well, your grades are not very good."

This guy is quite the genius, I thought. Yes, my grades were bad.

"What do you like to read," he asked. I am sure *Chaucer* or perhaps *War and Peace* would have been the right answer, but I blurted out "The Sporting News."

"I see you have a sense of humor, young man. We frown on that at Choate." I was not sure if he was kidding or not. Something told me the interview was not going well.

"What are your goals in life, David?" was the next question.

"Well, I want to play professional baseball," I said. At this point, my family history and earlier achievements of my older cousins were going down in flames.

"Well, Mr. and Mrs. Griswold, we have many qualified students applying, and we are limited in who we can accept. You will hear from us," said a frowning Mr. Bumble. That ended the interview.

The drive home from Choate was not great. "Is that the best you could do?" asked my father.

"Well, I didn't like him," was my reply.

My mother being from Kentucky, could not wait to get home and have a bourbon.

Realizing that Choate may not be the right school, I was scheduled to go to Hotchkiss, another fine prep school in Lakeville, Connecticut. As I was getting ready to go to

Hotchkiss, the letter with the expected result arrived from Choate. The letter read, David has wonderful potential but is young for his age, and his grades need to be improved, especially in English, math, science, and history. The only subjects that were deemed satisfactory were physical education and woodshop. David should apply next year. That was not going to happen.

With this defeat in mind and more coaching from my family, we went off to Hotchkiss. Similar results. The next school was Kent in Western Connecticut, a beautiful school. Kent has strong ties to the Episcopal Church. My mother was a devoted Episcopalian, and she held out high hopes that her devotion to that religion would bear fruit. However, her prayers for results were not to be.

"David needs more seasoning," said this headmaster as if he was examining a cantaloupe.

At this point, I should mention that my father's health was in rapid decline. He had rheumatic fever as a child, and his heart was failing. Today, he would have a valve replacement and go on for many more years. But that surgery was not yet perfected, and he was extremely sick. So, it was up to my mother to schedule and take me to more interviews. My Dad had turned his study into a war room with red pins stuck into maps of prep schools throughout Connecticut.

The next round included Loomis, Westminster, and Taft. Other relatives had gone to these schools and done well. Still, I was not able to ride in on their names. I laughed and said they must have really screwed up, but my humor was not going over too well. More rejections.

We had now dropped to another level. All were very good schools but without the name recognition of my earlier selections. Salisbury, Berkshire, Gunnery, South Kent, and

Pomfret were all visited. They all said no. At this point, it was decided that perhaps we should look out of state. St. Paul's in New Hampshire was targeted and then Andover, followed by Lenox in Massachusetts. They were consistent with the Connecticut schools in a unanimous consensus that I was not prep school material.

At this point, if you are keeping count, I had been rejected by fourteen schools and had developed a real hatred of all headmasters. To hell with all of them. I would play baseball, chase girls with Jimmy, and drive stock cars at the local racetrack. My poor mother was terribly disappointed. My father was becoming sicker, and my relatives were starting to come to grips that somehow there would be a Griswold that was not going to meet the expected standards. My cousins regarded me as some type of genetic mutant that had to be tolerated but kept at arm's length.

For my birthday, one for my cousins gave me a tool belt, which I am sure he thought was extremely funny. I had a great desire to beat him up, but he was bigger and stronger. My response was put on hold.

"I must be setting a record in rejections," I laughed, but underneath my self-confidence was eroding. My conclusion was that I wasn't very smart. This was accented by comparison to my father and two uncles, all who had excelled at Yale and gone on to establish successful careers. While they never said anything to me directly, I could see them speaking together and everyone shaking their heads. Again, I felt I was letting everyone down, particularly my father, whom I idolized.

C. Lambert Heyniger

Then my mother heard of a school in New Lebanon, New York, named The Darrow School. Since we had never interviewed in New York, she decided why not give it a shot. Once again, she and I got into the family car and drove to New Lebanon, New York. The trip took approximately three hours from our home. As we headed into the Berkshire Mountains, I began to identify with how cattle must feel riding to the Chicago Stockyards. This would be another negative interview followed by another rejection letter. It was only out of respect for my mother and to appease my extremely sick father that I was even in the car.

The school was located halfway up a mountain, and to reach it, you turned off the main road on to a dirt road. As we bounced along, we saw some old falling down buildings. I honestly thought we were going to a logging camp. Finally, we came to a clearing, and the school appeared. It was a far cry from the manicured lawns of Choate. As was the procedure, an upperclassman showed us around. It seemed the buildings were owned at one time by the Shakers. The Shakers were a group of men and women that resembled the Amish of Pennsylvania. I was not impressed. It appeared the Shakers had a rather strange belief that was more exotic than the Amish. That being, they did not believe in fraternizing with the opposite sex. As a result, they had a difficult time reproducing and ultimately died out as a group. It took me a moment for this to sink in.

"You mean," I said to our guide, "They did not have sex?"

"No," was the answer.

That settled it! No way was I going to this school. My mother could read my concerns.

"That was a long time ago, dear. I am sure the school does not hold on to those traditions."

I could only hope.

Now it was time to meet the headmaster, Mr. Heyniger. Mr. Heyniger had been a star salesman for the Cadillac division of General Motors. Destined for a senior position, the Chairman of the Board of General Motors, Alfred P. Sloan, had hand-selected Mr. Heyniger to come to Detroit and assume an important corporate role. However, Mr. Heyniger always wanted to have a school for boys, young men who needed a second chance in life. Alfred P. Sloan understood, and it was General Motors checks that had financed the dream of Mr. Heyniger. Thus Mr. Heyniger started his school in 1939. It was now 1959, and Mr. Heyniger was old. He was also very big. In fact, he was huge. Even bent over with age, he must have been at least 6'4". His body and head were large, but what really stood out were his hands. They resembled the paws of a small bear or a large dinner plate. I was beginning to reconsider how I would react to the next questions regarding his school.

Mr. Heyniger talked with my mother. Mr. Heyniger mentioned he had graduated from Princeton, and my mother quickly mentioned her father was a Princeton man. Despite that plus, I just sat there waiting for the predictable outcome. Finally, he turned to me and asked the question I knew was coming.

"David, would you like to come to my school?"

I was contemplating the answer, which would be no, but I was not sure how to phrase it. I could imagine one of those giant bear paws knocking me across the room if I was too rude in my reply. As I pondered my response to his question, my mother kicked me under the table, and I blurted out, "I guess so."

I guess so was the best I could manage. At that point, most any school administrator would have launched into the-we have many applicants speech, and that would have ended the interview. But not Mr. Heyniger. He just looked at me. It was as if he was staring right through me. I was becoming extremely uncomfortable as he continued to stare. Finally, he turned to my mother.

"Mrs. Griswold," he stated in his deep voice, "David does not have the grades we normally look for, but I believe in this young man, and I want him to come to my school."

My mother looked like she was going to faint.

"You mean he is accepted? Isn't there a need to discuss the matter with others?" she asked.

Mr. Heyniger smiled. "I make the decision at this school. David is accepted."

I was stunned. I was so prepared for rejection that I was speechless. I think I finally said thank you. It wasn't until we were in the car headed back to Connecticut that I realized what had happened. This kind older man had looked beyond the grades and beyond the face of a very scared young man. Instead, he had seen something in my eyes that other headmasters had failed to see. He saw the great desire to be someone and to meet my family's traditions. He believed in me when no one else had. I vowed to work hard and make him proud. He would die within the year, and I never forgot him or the faith he had in me. I have always tried to live up to his expectations.

**C. Lambert Heyniger
The Darrow School Headmaster**

My Dad

The summer disappeared, and September began. It was time to go to The Darrow School. Again, I had mixed emotions about leaving my high school friends, but I did not want to disappoint my family. I was coming to grips with the reality that prep school might not be too bad. My Dad was home from the hospital and resting comfortably. I went in to see him in his bedroom.

"I know you will do well. I am proud of you," he said.

"Thank you. I will try," I said. "You and Mom will come up for parent's weekend and see me. You will be better then."

My Dad managed to smile. "Come here," he said. I walked over to the bed, and he hugged me. "I love you."

Somewhat embarrassed, I said, "sure, sure," and walked out.

"Dad's getting better, right?" I asked my mother. She attempted a weak smile but said nothing.

Leaving my Dad and entering Darrow, I was propelled into a quite different world. High school was pretty laid back. You wanted to do well, but there was little pressure. The dress was casual, jeans and sport shirts or pullovers. There were many options for studies. English and American History were required, but after that, you could choose anything from college preparatory to agriculture to woodshop or auto mechanics. But the biggest factor was my free time. After the school day ended, you were on your own. Sports, cars, hanging around a soda shop, TV, and of course, dating, which involved talking on the phones for hours and a great deal of time riding around in the evenings. Careers were not discussed. Some went to college, some to the military, but most went to work. One option was the local manufacturing plants. Big companies like General Dynamics, Pfizer, General Electric, and a host of smaller manufacturing plants were prevalent. Others went into the trades. Many had fathers who worked or owned businesses in carpentry, plumbing, electrical, or automotive. For most high school graduates, the path was clear. Get a job in the area, marry your high school sweetheart, have children, and settle down. There was nothing wrong with those choices, but it did not require a great deal of planning. It just happened.

Prep school was vastly different. You wore a tie and jacket to class, and on Sunday, you wore a dark suit to chapel service and Sunday lunch. Classes were very structured, with very few electives—everything geared towards college admissions. After classes, you had two hours of sports, and then you went to dinner. After dinner, you went to the study hall, and after study hall, you went to bed. There were no radios, TVs, phones, cars, or girls to distract you from learning. The goal of everyone was to go to college and not just any college.

To some extent, the college choice was geared to your interests. Those interested in engineering targeted MIT. Those interested in medicine targeted John Hopkins, Finance, Wharton, foreign language, Middlebury. The first question I was asked when I arrived at Darrow was what college I was interested in attending. I had never given it any thought. I had concentrated on sports and girls in high school. My reply to the question from my new prep school friends was "Yale."

"Really, Yale. You better get good grades."

I had never given grades much thought. No one at family dinners talked about grades. Grades must be for others. Griswold's went to Yale. Prep school would be an introduction to cold reality.

Along with a very structured environment that I desperately needed, the best part of prep school was the friends I made. Most were highly successful in their life, and it has been wonderful staying in touch with them over the years. I always look forward to reunions where we can catch up and trade stories on our experiences. But of all the friends I made, one stands out. His name is Bob Lang. He was from New Jersey, and we would become lifelong friends. He was a street-smart kid who knew the ropes. I had never met anyone like him. He talked fast and brought an intense energy level to conversations where ideas and thoughts appeared to spring from him like a Roman Candle. He immediately had a rundown on all the masters (teachers). He took me under his wing and guided me into taking courses that I could pass. We both enjoyed sports. He quarterbacked the football team, played baseball, and captained the hockey team. He was an exceptional hockey player and would get a scholarship to play hockey in Denver. I played soccer, basketball, and baseball. We roomed together and not only enjoyed sports, but our family backgrounds were similar. His family had been successful and had fallen on hard times. There were many parallels to my situation.

In later life, he would go on to set sales records in the insurance business with his aggressive style, boundless energy, and a real mastery of numbers. His success in the insurance industry was a combination of charm, style, and talking so fast most had no idea what they were buying. But people liked him, and he did know the products. His success in sales led to an opportunity to fulfill one of his greatest loves, which was horse racing. Since my mother had lived in Lexington, Kentucky, I too shared enjoyment of racing. Together we would travel to Keeneland in Kentucky,

Gulfstream in Florida, and Saratoga in New York. With his skill with numbers, he was an excellent handicapper and would place bets with a good chance of winning. For me, it was more the spectacle of the track, the beauty of the thoroughbred horses, and the fascinating people one would meet. We even went in on a horse together, and it won a race at Belmont in New York. Standing in the winners' circle was a real thrill for me. He is a wonderful friend, and it all started at Darrow.

T. Harry "Bob" Lang

Along with forming many lifetime friendships, I did make the varsity soccer team and was liked by the upperclassmen. This was not so bad, after all. The professors in the classroom liked my effort and had not yet realized what an academic challenge they had on their hands. It was all going well. I had been at school for six weeks and really getting to enjoy the experience. That would change overnight.

I remember the day. It was around noon, and I was in a study hall trying to understand an algebra problem. Suddenly out of nowhere, Mr. Nunley appeared. Mr. Nunley was a very stern Master who taught English to upperlevel students. I was a little intimidated by him.

"Pick up your books and come with me," said Mr. Nunley. *Lord, what have I done now?*

I had been late to class earlier in the week, and perhaps I was going to get a lecture and maybe some demerits. I followed Mr. Nunley into the headmaster's office. No one was there, but a phone was on his desk, and it was off the hook.

"The call is for you," stated Mr. Nunley, and he quickly disappeared. I picked up the phone.

"David, this is Grandma."

"Hi Grandma, are you planning on coming up with Mom and Dad for parent's weekend?"

There was a long pause. "David, your Dad died last night. Your cousin Lea will be coming within the hour to get you and bring you home. We love you and will see you soon."

I was speechless. I put down the phone. Mr. Nunley reappeared.

"I am sorry," he said. "Follow me."

Later, people said I was in shock. I said nothing; no tears, no emotions, just stunned silence. I was led over to my dorm, where a senior helped me pack my suitcase. I then went downstairs to wait for my cousin. The school Chaplin came over and offered some words of comfort, but I honestly do not remember one word.

Lea arrived, and I got in the car. He was perhaps the kindest of all the cousins and by far the best choice for this trip. Lea immediately realized I was in no shape to talk, and we drove to Connecticut in silence. As we got near my hometown, he said, "Your Dad was a fine man," and I said, "thank you." That is all I remember.

The funeral was the next day. The beautiful old church was packed as my Dad was extremely popular. Not only were all the proper members of the community present, but all his workers and many local citizens were there as well. The Griswold family occupied the first five pews in the church. Again, I remember nothing except for one moment. I turned around during the service and saw my two uncles. Their usual stern looks were gone, and tears were running down their cheeks. One reached out and put his hand on my shoulder. It was a small but such a meaningful gesture. I remember it well.

The next day my mother and I were alone. I recall walking out in the backyard where my Dad played ball with me. I could see him standing there, hitting those baseballs with his bleeding hands. He had a skin disease called eczema, and his skin was cracked and bleeding as he continued to grip a bat. Mother would tell him to stop, but he delighted in seeing me do well. He would continue until the bat was covered in blood. I never realized until then how much he loved me. Standing there in the yard, I knew I would never see him again. The tears fell.

I walked back inside. My mother entered the room and could tell I had been crying. I looked up at her.

"Why?" I asked. His brothers were healthy and would live for another 25 years. Why him?

It was at that time that my mother said the words that I would remember for a lifetime.

"Death," my mother said, pausing to gather her words, "death is permanent, you must accept it. Some things can be changed, but death is not one of them. Remember the Lord's prayer-...thy kingdom come; thy will be done. It is His will. We may not understand it, but we must accept it."

I remembered so little of the funeral, but I never forgot that message. How fortuitous that just seven short years later, halfway around the world in a country that most Americans had never heard of, those words would provide comfort for me and offer support to those I was destined to lead.

Prep School

Returning to Darrow after the funeral, I quickly got into the routine. I continued to play on the varsity soccer team and would become captain of the baseball team. But the classroom was a different story—more C's and D's. Much later, I was diagnosed with attention deficit syndrome (ADD). Still, back then, I was diagnosed as lazy and not motivated. The truth was I was very motivated to meet my family's expectations. Still, my interest in girls, sports, and fast cars often derailed my concentration. Also, I developed a taste for beer. Those interests, combined with my inability to stay focused for an extended period, produced more below-average grades.

Nevertheless, the three years flew by, and it was the spring of 1962. I was preparing to graduate. The burning question for all of us was, where would we go to college? I met with Mr. Nunley, the same man who had taken me to the phone call from my grandmother. Mr. Nuley was well versed in colleges, and he had his favorites. Since his undergraduate work was at Dartmouth, the Ivy League was selected for the very brightest students. Next in line was commonly referred to as the "Little Three"-Amherst, Williams, and Wesleyan. Mr. Nunley also thought highly of the Maine schools- Bowdoin, Bates, and Colby. Other favorites were Hobart, Middlebury, and William and Mary. Most state schools were looked on with disdain with one notable exception. Mr. Nunley loved the University of Virginia, and several Darrow students always went there. It is worth mentioning that none of these schools were put on my list.

My meeting with Mr. Nunley was less than inspiring.

"Where do you want to go, David?" he asked.

"Well, all my family goes to Yale," I said with a smile.

"Well, David, apparently not all of them." He paused to let that sink in. "Let us be serious. Yale accepts less than 10% of applicants, and their applicants come from the top percentage of students around the country. Sending your application to Yale would damage my credibility as a guidance counselor," he said with a slight smile. I never knew if he was mean, or it was his very stiff upper lipped sense of humor.

"I have a good school for you," Mr. Nunley continued.

Mr. Nunley had selected Gettysburg College in Gettysburg, Pennsylvania, as my first choice. I never heard of it. All I knew was President Eisenhower had a farm there, and I guess that would please my Republican family.

"Now, David, any realistic thoughts?" The emphasis was on realistic.

"Well, Coach Mahken my baseball coach, went to Springfield College."

"Springfield is a fine school since you like sports. It will be put on the list," said Mr. Nunley with about as much enthusiasm as he could muster for a student who was clearly a challenge.

"However," I continued, "I really want to go to Rollins College in Winter Park, Florida."

"Rollins," exclaimed Mr. Nunley, who had no respect for education in the deep South.

"Why, Rollins?"

"Well," I replied, "Rollins has a good baseball team, warm weather, and it is on a beautiful lake with Spanish moss on the trees."

"Ah yes," said Mr. Nunley "Spanish moss is quite essential to achievement in higher education. I see you have put much thought into your future."

God, he could be sarcastic. He did, however, give me the applications, and I sent them to the three schools.

Gettysburg replied that I would have to go to summer school and improve my math grades. If that happened, I would be put on the waiting list. Not a ringing endorsement as it was highly doubtful my math scores would ever improve. Springfield said yes thanks mostly to Coach Mahken, who called in some favors from his old alma mater and drove me down for a personal interview. He was a wonderful man and really looked after me. And then to my pleasant surprise, Rollins said yes. Rollins was my choice. Baseball, warm weather, beautiful girls on the lake, and of course, Spanish moss. I was all set. There was only one problem.

In our small town, there was one Curtis Harrington. Curtis was married, sort of. Thanks to a very generous trust fund, Curtis could put his wife into a beautiful home with cars, clothes, and social standing. In return for this benefit, Curtis felt he could trade off on not taking his marriage vows too seriously. In other words, Curtis had affairs, many of them. His wife had to know as the whole town was aware of Curtis's infidelity. However, not wanting to change her standard of living, she looked the other way and continued to remain in the proper social circles. But in quiet conversations, the infidelities of Curtis Harrington were often discussed. People often asked what led him astray. It could not have been the family. The Harrington's were from good families with proper backgrounds. They were well-liked and very wealthy, which was never lost on the social set.

My mother played bridge with the elder Mrs. Harrington. No, it was not the family. Curtis had a brother, and he was a fine upstanding citizen. Married with a great job and a member of the country club, Curtis's brother, was an excellent golfer and club champion two years in a row. No, it was not his brother, who exemplified proper behavior. Therefore, it was concluded that the cause of Curtis Harrington's debauchery was the college he had attended. Yes, it was a college that led poor Curtis astray. And the college was none other than Rollins. I could not believe it. Of all the colleges in the country, and the Harringtons could have bought Curtis into any of them, it was Rollins. What were the odds?

"You are not turning out like Curtis Harrington," was my mother's decree.

Other family members nodded their heads. Therefore, the family decided that Springfield College would be the choice. Since they were paying for my education, I had no input, and arguing with family members was twenty-five years off. One accepted the family dictates of those times without question.

Springfield was not Yale. News of my not going to Yale traveled fast around Griswold Point, the enclave that housed most of our family. My college choice was not well received. In fact, if I had been sent to a reformatory, it could not have been any worse.

"A Griswold not at Yale-it has never happened," stated my aunt, who resembled and acted much like Miss PittyPat in *Gone with the Wind*. Miss PittyPat was a grand dame of a well-heeled Georgia family who was famous in the movie classic for saying:

"Yankees in Georgia-whoever let them in?".

My proud uncles shook their heads in disbelief. My mother blamed the entire educational system, which had failed her son. It was disappointing, but I was prepared to make the best of it and do well at Springfield.

My First Car

To go to college, I would need a car. Springfield was an hour and a half from where I lived. I had obtained my license but always drove my mother's car during the summer.

Money was tight since my Dad's death, so I set my sights on a very used car in a dealership in a nearby town. I went with my old friend from high school, Jimmy Falcone, to look over the cars on the lot. Neither-one-of us knew much about cars. Our most important criteria for selection was what would impress girls. With that in mind, we selected an old Ford that had a sky roof. It was like sunroofs of today. However, the roof was not retractable. It was just a plastic top and thus the name; Skyliner.

"This is great, Gris," said my buddy, Jimmy.

"You can be parking with a hot date and look up at the stars. It will be romantic, and with that setting, you can't miss." I must admit he had a great pitch.

With that glowing promise in mind, I bought the car without any consideration of such mundane things as engines, transmissions, tires, or brakes. I don't think I even looked under the hood. Not that it would have made much difference. All I could think of was who I would call for the first date in the Skyliner.

I drove the car home, and my mother was impressed with my first major purchase. It seemed like a good car. Well, it was for about two weeks. Then things started to go wrong, very wrong. Oil was disappearing, pushed over 50 miles per hour the whole car would shake, and strange noises were coming from the engine, sort of an ominous knocking sound. Concerned, I took it to a mechanic in our town who had known my father. He was a nice man and a particularly good mechanic.

"This is a disaster," was his first remark. He then ticked off a series of problems.

"How much to fix it?" I asked.

His price was twice what I paid for it. He then added: "Honestly, it isn't worth it. I would junk it for parts and start over."

I was devastated. I had spent all the money I had to buy the car and had nothing left to repair it, much less buy another car. I had no idea what to do, and my mother was in no position to help.

During this frustrating time, one of my uncles stopped by. He did this regularly to check on us. He noted I was rather depressed.

"What's wrong, David?" he asked.

"I bought this car, and it is a total wreck. I can't drive it anywhere, and I need it for college," I replied.

"David," said my stern uncle, "Did you have a mechanic check it out?"

"No, I just like how it looked."

"David, you must be more responsible. This was a terrible decision. You spent what little money you have on a car without having it checked out."

"Yes sir," I managed to say feeling like a total failure.

"Let this be a lesson," he said and promptly disappeared.

If I had felt badly before, I felt even worse now. Of course, my uncle was right, and I had failed again to meet family standards. I had no idea what to do next.

A week passed with no resolution to the car when the phone rang.

"Is Mr. Griswold there?" came the voice on the other end.

I was puzzled. My father, Mr. Griswold, had been dead for three years. "I am sorry, but Mr. Griswold passed away some time ago," I answered.

"Mr. David Griswold," came the reply.

"I am David Griswold," I said. No one had ever called me Mr. Griswold.

"Mr. David Griswold, this is the General Manager at the dealership where you bought a car."

"Yes," I answered.

"Mr. Griswold, could you bring the car up to our dealership?"

"Sure," I said. I hoped the car could make it.

Upon my arrival at the dealership, I was met by the General Manager, who introduced me to the President. I had no idea why they wanted to speak with me.

"Mr. Griswold," said the President. "There has been a terrible mistake. I understand you are having problems with the car we sold you."

"Yes, it has several problems," I said in a rather subdued tone.

"Well, we pride ourselves on happy customers. Here is what we are prepared to do. We will take back this car and give you another one, a year newer and with lower mileage, at no additional charge. Further, if you have any problems, just call us. We will take care of it."

"Gosh, thank you," I said. I still had no idea what was happening.

I drove the car home, and it was a much better car. I walked into the house and spoke to my mother.

"Strangest thing just happened," and I told her what had transpired. "Can you believe it; they just gave me a better car."

My mother said, "That is strange. I guess they are simply good people."

It took me a long time to finally put it all together and figure out what had happened. I approached my uncle with the story of my trip to the dealership.

"You don't say. That is strange," he volunteered. "Just remember to check things out before you buy them."

I agreed and asked if he had anything to do with what had happened.

"I have no idea what you mean," he said with a slight smile.

Much later, the story was confirmed. My uncle told the dealership to make right by me or never consider selling another car in our town. My uncles had that kind of influence and power.

I learned a valuable lesson and came to appreciate the way my family conducted business. Instead of saying sure, I will take care of it, my uncle had stressed responsibility. Then after he resolved the issue, instead of bragging about his power and authority, he declined to take credit, content in the outcome.

College Years

In looking back at college, my first year was by far the most difficult. I had selected education with an emphasis on physical education as my major, mostly because I liked sports. To earn that degree, Springfield emphasized the sciences - botany, zoology, anatomy, physiology, and physiology of exercise. These were hard courses, and I managed to flunk one of them in my first year. To get back in good standing, it would be required that I go to summer school to make up the course I had flunked. This was rather humiliating. Not only did I not get into Yale, but now I was in danger of flunking out of Springfield. I hated summer school and was beginning to wonder if college was the right path.

To make matters worse, the summer school was past New Haven, and I had to drive by Yale to get to my class. I could just envision my family elders shaking their heads as I passed the school of choice and went into the parking lot of a state university. I was full of self-doubts regarding education, and at the same time, I was being torn in two directions from a social standpoint.

On one side was my family and my upperclass friends. I would go to the beach club to swim and the country club to play tennis. I would dress in the prescribed manner of loafers, no socks, Bermuda shorts or white slacks and polo shirts for these occasions. The drink of choice at the club was a gin and tonic with a lime. Another favorite was an Old Fashion made with bourbon, of course. Conversations consisted of colleges, politics, and business. I enjoyed the clubs, and my family's reputation was very helpful. Everyone was genuinely nice to me.

However, I also liked my old high school friends. I would slip into jeans, boots, and a tee-shirt and enter a very different world. Activities included the stock car track in the next town. The people at the stock car track were far removed from those at the clubs. But the races were exciting, and I liked the roar of the engines and the competition. Another pastime was shooting rats at the town dump. We all had .22 rifles, and we would park at the dump, load the rifles, and when we turned on the car lights, the rats would be seen running over the garbage. We would shoot them, which was great fun. The drink of choice was beer, and we enjoyed a few cans as we exterminated the rodents.

While there were differences in hanging out with my family friends and my town friends in terms of clothing, style, conversations, and alcohol, the greatest difference was the girls. As mentioned, my mother grew up in Kentucky among the beautiful horse farms where there was an emphasis on breeding. Mother wanted her only son to be "bred" to the right person. Up the road from where we lived was a large home belonging to the Wentworths. Mr. Wentworth had inherited a small fortune and spent most of his time fishing. The summer and fall, he trolled the waters of Connecticut. In the winters and early spring, he fished the waters of their other home in Sarasota, Florida. He sat on a couple of corporate boards, but that did not require much time and did not interfere with fishing. His wife was a lovely woman who played golf and contributed much of her time to charity work at the local Episcopal church. It was at church that she met my mother, and they struck up a strong friendship. The Wentworth's had a daughter named Cynthia, but everyone called her Sissie. Sissie Wentworth was very proper, polite, cultured, and had a trust fund. My mother felt it was a perfect match. A courtship was arranged.

I would see Sissie at arranged club functions, and everyone thought we were a perfect couple. Often, we would meet at each other homes for cookouts or TV watching. I remember one of those meetings. Driving up to the Wentworth's home, I parked in their circular driveway and stepped up on their porch supported by six large ionic columns. Opening the large door, I entered a beautiful foyer where a large crystal chandelier hung. The living room was off to the right. It was tastefully furnished with very stylish wallpaper. Oil paintings of family members hung on the walls and a lovely picture of Sissie when she was around ten, was centered over the large fireplace. Mr. and Mrs. Wentworth welcomed me and led me into the den, which was off the living room. The den was walled in dark mahogany with pictures of boats and fish. In fact, there was a giant sailfish mounted on one wall. Quite sporty.

"Great to see you, David," said Mr. Wentworth.

Thank you, sir," I responded.

"How is your mother?" asked Mrs. Wentworth.

"Just fine, thank you," I said.

"Well, please give her our best."

"Would you like something to drink?" asked Mrs. Wentworth. "A coke or a ginger ale?"

Since mixed drinks or beer were definitely not on the menu, I settled for a coke, and Mrs. Wentworth was off to bring two cokes on a silver tray with crackers and cheese. Sissie appeared in tan slacks and a pretty blue sweater with her initials monogrammed on the front. She and I settled in to watch TV. As I recall, we watched *I Love Lucy* or *Leave It to Beaver* - two of the more popular shows of the day. Mr.

Wentworth kept the door slightly open to be sure nothing inappropriate happened. Not that there was any chance of that happening. The truth was that as nice and pleasant as Sissie was, she did not excite me. I found her pleasant, but the conversation was forced around weather and schools, and there was no desire for a physical relationship. At around 9:30, Mr. Wentworth announced it was time for Sissie to get her beauty sleep, and I said my goodbyes and maybe kissed her on the cheek; I really do not recall. I left their home, got into my car, and headed down their very long driveway. At that point, my car was supposed to turn left and head south to the shore where our home was located. But instead, as if by some magnetic force, my car turned right, and headed north into the blue collar section of town and to the modest home of Sal and Marie DeCarlo. The DeCarlo home was a single level three-bedroom ranch. It consisted of a small living room, a smaller breakfast nook, and a tiny kitchen. Three small bedrooms were off the living room. The entire house could fit in the Wentworth's living room.

Mr. DeCarlo was a part-time carpenter, and Mrs. DeCarlo, a seamstress. They had one daughter, Donna. Donna DeCarlo had blond hair and blue eyes, much like Sissie. The likeness ended there. Sissie had a somewhat pale complexion and wore just the slightest touch of makeup. It was all in particularly good taste. Donna had the darker skin of her southern Mediterranean Sicilian heritage. She wore a great amount of makeup that included fake eyelashes, heavy eyeliner, and a great amount of eye shadow. In fact, in the dark, she could have been mistaken for a raccoon. But the real difference was below the neck. To put it as politely as possible, Donna was well endowed, and rather than hide her ample assets, Donna wore the tightest clothes possible. While

Sissie had very tailored clothes from Lord and Taylor, Donna did her shopping at Frederick's of Hollywood.

Arriving at the DeCarlo's, I was greeted by Marie DeCarlo, who hugged me and thanked me for coming over. She then informed me that she and Sal would be going out for a few hours. Sal seemed surprised with that announcement but went along. '

"David," said Marie, "There is plenty of beer in the refrigerator and spaghetti on the stove. Feel free to help yourself."

Donna just smiled and told her mother to take her time getting home.

So, after my evening of Coca-Cola and brie at the Wentworths, I found myself drinking beer, eating spaghetti, and starring at Donna's skintight sweater that was complimented by a noticeably short leather mini skirt. As I consumed my meal, I continued to stare at Donna, who sat across from me with a wonderful habit of crisscrossing her legs and arching her back. This had the desired effect.

"Would you like another beer?" asked Donna.

"That would be great," I said as I watched Donna sashay into the kitchen.

It was on the way back from the kitchen with my beer that Donna apparently felt her clothing was too restrictive; so, by the time she had entered the living room, she was clad only in a small bra that was straining to fulfill its mission of support and a pair of black lace panties. Pausing for effect, Donna smiled and said,

"Would you like to see my bedroom?"

Like many young men of my age group, I struggled with some of the complex teachings of the church. However, at that moment, as I stared at Donna and processed her invitation, there was absolutely, unequivocally, no doubt in my mind whatsoever that there was a God.

As the summer progressed, I found myself living in two different worlds. The social clubs one day and the town dump the next. Sissie and her upscale parents one day. The voluptuous Donna and her complicit parents the next. While this may seem like a great life, it caused me some concerns. While I enjoyed both situations, I really did not fit into either of them. While I liked my club friends, I found some of them to be snobby, and in some cases, they had an extremely poor work ethic. Flush with money, the idea of work was to plan parties, schedule family events, and have long discussions with the brokers who oversaw their trust funds. On the other hand, my high school friends were limited in their goals and ambitions. The truth was, I was well received in both groups but not totally accepted by either.

One thing I did notice was, the two groups never mixed. Never. I was kind of aware of that fact, but I was about to test that unwritten rule. This was not one of my better decisions. The setting was the annual Labor Day dance at the country club. All the proper people would be there, and I was expected to bring Sissie Wentworth. However, I thought this would be a great time to introduce Donna DeCarlo to high society. I asked Donna to the Labor Day Dance at the club. She accepted with great enthusiasm, and the DeCarlo's, who were devout Catholics, lit a candle.

The holiday arrived, and everyone was dressed to the nines. The ladies all had beautiful cotillion type dresses, and the gentlemen all sported dark suits. Donna was extremely excited and dressed for the occasion. With an added amount of makeup, she wore a lowcut sequined blouse that accented her greatest assets. She had selected a skirt so tight that she could barely walk. The ensemble was topped off with bright red stiletto heels.

When we walked into the dance, everyone noticed us immediately, and I was basking in the attention.

"Way to go, Gris," said some of my male friends.

Others just stared in disbelief. The young ladies had a quite different reaction. They had daggers in their eyes and had looks on their faces that would suggest they had just had a drink of sour milk. As the dance progressed, and everyone fox trotted and waltzed around the floor, Donna offered a version of dancing that had never been seen at the club. As the evening came to a conclusion and the band played the traditional Stardust song- "And now the purple shades of twilight time," and everyone danced cheek to cheek, Donna threw her arms around my neck, ground her hips into me, and proceeded to French kiss me. One of the chaperones, Mrs. Charles Raynor Roosevelt, a direct descendant of old T.R., appeared to faint. I thought it was a hell of an evening.

The next morning, I strolled downstairs to meet my mother.

"'How could you," was her first comment. "Have you lost your mind?" followed. "My friends all had their children at that dance. The Ely's, Bingham's, Patterson's, Ludington's, Marshes, Harrington's, how will I face them? Mrs. Wentworth has called. Poor dear Sissie has been crying her eyes out. What were you thinking?"

"Well," I stammered, "I just thought."

"You thought!" cried my mother.

"You don't understand."

"Understand, of course, I understand. You were not brought by the stork. Of course, I understand, but there is a time and a place and with the right people."

My mother was so upset she fell back on her Kentucky horse farm analogy.

"Good God, David, the thoroughbreds do not run all over the farm. That's why they have fences."

At that moment, I had to smile, thinking of my family building a large fence around the town to keep me in the right pasture. My mother did not appreciate the smile. It was time to bring out the big guns.

"David, you have a responsibility to your family. That is your father's signet ring you are wearing. It has meaning. Not only have you embarrassed our family and yourself, but you are not being fair to that girl. You have no intention of marrying her, and you are just going to hurt her as well as a lot of other people."

I knew she was right, and I was beginning to see her point. I said I was sorry, and I was.

"Well," sighed my mother, "You have a slow learning curve," but then she smiled, "You do know how to have fun."

That's what I loved about her, she had made her point and then left me with a smile.

After the Labor Day dance, I returned to Springfield and became more involved in college life. I stayed in Springfield on the weekends, and Donna slipped into the past. I worked hard at school, played soccer and baseball, and the academics became easier. The years flew by, and three years later, I would graduate from Springfield College with a bachelor's degree in Science. In retrospect, I really should have gotten a Bachelor of Arts. I enjoyed English and excelled in composition thanks to my training at Darrow. Also, I enjoyed history, especially the essays where I would write about national leaders and how they accomplished various goals.

On the other side, I struggled with science courses. I recall Anatomy and Physiology, where I had to dissect a large cat. The exams would have pins stuck in various muscles, and you would have to identify them. Apparently, identifying the hind leg and the paw was not what they were looking for. I was given a D for showing up. Another problem occurred in my sophomore year. Springfield required you take a course in religion. Today, they would probably bulldoze the school for such a requirement, but this was the early 60's, and no one questioned the rules. All my roommates took Christianity. It was a ridiculously easy course, and everyone got an A. The final exam was multiple choice with questions like Jesus was A a plumber, B a dentist, C the son of God, or D a banker. It was a home run. But for some unknown reason, I decided to broaden my education and take religions of the world. I was the only physical education major in a class of deep thinking theologians. We studied Buddhism, Taoism, Hinduism, and about 10 other isms. I was lost from the start, and the professor compared me to a lamb of biblical days that had strayed from the flock. Again, they generously gave me a D. As a result of questionable courses, my grade point average hovered around 2.0. If it fell below that, I would not graduate. It was now my senior year, and I was getting nervous.

In the winter, it was time to go out, and student teach. We would be expected to teach classes in schools in the Northeast that were serious about physical education. You had to prepare lesson plans and would be graded by a team of teachers. I was not comfortable with this approach. Therefore, I came up with a great idea. Why not do my student teaching in Florida? Warm weather and a little less stress on the program. The head of the student teaching program said if we could get ten people, he would authorize it. All my roommates and six others jumped at the opportunity. We were off to Florida.

I taught at a high school in Palmetto, Florida. Palmetto is just north of Bradenton on the west coast and nestled up against the Sunshine Skyway Bridge. It is a beautiful little town, and the school welcomed me with open arms. I got along great with the students in my classes, but my real joy was coaching the baseball team. We won our first five games, and I was coming to the realization that while I was struggling in the classroom, I could relate to others. The players responded to my coaching advice, and the head coach saw some potential. I received an A in student teaching and moved my GPA to a solid 2.2. I graduated.

I recall the graduation ceremony in the spring of 1966. My mother hugged me and told me she was proud of me. She added that she was sure my Dad was proud, too, and that brought a tear to my eye. One of my aunts attended and immediately brought me back to earth. She was dressed in a beautiful Saks Fifth Avenue suit with a mink stole. Totally out of place, but it did raise some eyebrows. She kissed me on the cheek and said:

"Well, we need teachers too."

I thanked her for coming and let the comment roll off as I was used to it by this time.

My three college roommates were there, of course, with their families and friends. Big groups. All proud of the fact that their sons would be professional teachers and coaches. I was happy for them but must admit I was a little envious. My family was not that impressed with my chosen field.

Now I should say here that Springfield College is an excellent school. Steeped in the humanities, Springfield has produced excellent teachers, coaches, trainers, and social workers. In fact, it was recently selected as one of the top 20 small colleges in America by US News and World Report. I was fortunate to go there. I learned a great deal, enjoyed playing sports, and made lifelong friends. I can say I am proud to be an alumnus.

However, my graduation from Springfield was not celebrated by my relatives. It was not Yale, and I felt like a failure. Again, I had let down the family. That feeling was only reinforced when, at a large family gathering, my stern Uncle congratulated my older cousins for their accomplishments and then turned to me asking:

"And David, what college is it you attended?" All to the laugher of the group.

At that moment, I had a great desire to show them all that I could do something very different and very special. I would join the military. But why did I pick the Marines? It is a question that I have been asked often. There were other branches of military service, and as a college graduate with a degree in education, I could have gotten a deferment and gone into teaching. All my college roommates did. So why join the Marines?

Understand, Griswold's had served in the military all the way back to the Revolutionary War. Still, like Yale, there was only one branch to be considered. Since most Griswold's sailed their small yachts in the summer around the Connecticut coast, the Navy was the obvious choice. My dad had served in the Navy, along with his brother and my many cousins. I would consider the Navy, but why not go one step further. No Griswold had ever joined the Marine Corps. One family member had served in the Army, and one cousin had even joined the Air Force. Still, the Marines were far too dangerous for men who felt their value to the country could not put them in harm's way. Getting shot was considered bad form and not in keeping with family tradition. Therefore, since I was the first not to go to Yale-what, the hell-I would be the first to join the Marines. That would show them.

Motivation

However, in full disclosure, my family's horror at my college selection, and my career path was not the only reason I was considering the Marines.

Up the road from where I lived was an absolutely gorgeous girl from a family that would meet my relatives' approval. Blond hair, blue eyes, and possessing a dynamite figure, she was breathtakingly beautiful. She rode horses, loved to swim, play golf at the club, and had a joyous laugh combined with a seductive stare. I was mesmerized by her and wanted her badly. It was my goal to win her affection and to accomplish this feat, I needed to gain the respect of her parents.

Her father was a retired Marine Major. After much effort, I finally secured a date with her and got to meet the Major. Like all Marines, he was confident and proud.

"What are your future plans?" asked the Major.

"Well, Sir, I am thinking of going into the service."

"I see," said the Major. "And what branch of the service?"

"It's between the Navy and the Marines," I said.

"Well, hell, son," replied the Major "That's no choice at all. Anyone worthy of dating my daughter better be a Marine. Here, have a drink."

The Major liked to drink, which hardly lowered his standing in my eyes. Drinking beers with the Major and listening to tales of Marine conquests in the hills of Korea was enchanting. Often, after many drinks, the Major would come out with statements such as:

"There were 200 Chinese coming at us, and we killed 400."

I would roar with laughter and see myself following in those footsteps, mowing down the hapless enemy. It was a great sales pitch. However, the Major's sales pitch was nothing compared to his daughter.

As we sat in my car, overlooking Long Island Sound, and engaged in what was commonly referred to back then as Submarine Race Watching, she said,

"You know, I just love men in those Marine dress blue uniforms. You would look great in one."

Then she whispered something that sealed my fate. "You would look even better getting out of one."

At that moment, the Navy had no chance.

Induction

So, with this history behind me, and with my college years ending, it was decision time. What to do next. The year was 1966, and Vietnam had gone from a small advisory situation to a very serious war. The Marines had landed a year earlier in Danang, a coastal city in the northern part of South Vietnam, and the Army followed into the southern regions of the country. The draft was in full force to meet the growing manpower requirements not only for Vietnam but to fulfill our obligations all over the world. President Kennedy was dead, and President Lyndon Johnson was determined to show Americas' strength. He was equally determined to support the defense industry that would be building all forms of military equipment, not only to supply the needs of the troops but to enhance the bottom line. It was never said that old Lyndon did not like bottomed lined profits.

Getting drafted as a private did not seem like a good idea, and going into teaching had lost its appeal. Then there was my family history and the invitation of the Major's daughter. With all this on my mind, I went downtown with my three college roommates to the induction center. I suppose you could call it job hunting.

My three college roommates were great guys, and we shared much in common. All had been excellent high school athletes.

Rick was a standout in soccer, basketball, and baseball. He was a particularly good baseball pitcher and would have pitched in college if he had not hurt his back in his sophomore year. He was extremely organized and would go on to be a highly successful teacher and basketball coach. Jim played football and track in high school and ran track in college. His easygoing nature was ideal for teaching and coaching at the junior high school level. He would go on to earn his doctorate degree. Skip was a little different. Even though he was small, he had tremendous hand-eye coordination. He was the starting high school quarterback, basketball guard, and shortstop on the baseball team. But it was golf where he excelled. He had won tournaments all over New England and was by far the best golfer at the college, where he was elected captain of the team. He was happy go lucky and never seemed to get upset over anything. Also, he was a math major, and his ability to calculate numbers made him a great poker player. Today, he is comped at Vegas to be in poker tournaments.

We had lived off-campus in an old beat-up apartment and enjoyed our time together. They had all accepted teaching assignments and thought it odd that I was not doing the same. However, if I wanted to go into the military, so be it. The real impact of Vietnam had not yet hit American campuses. In fact, most of us were not even sure where it was. Somewhere over in Asia was the common response. When asked why we were there, our answer was equally vague. Stop the communists was the answer-I guess.

As my roommates drank beer and ate grinders-subway sandwiches by today's reference point-I entered the induction center. Out of deference to my father and all the Griswolds, I felt an obligation to speak with the Navy. I entered the Navy recruiting office.

"Welcome," said the naval officer. "Looking to join up?" he said with a smile. He was very friendly. "I am considering it," I said.

"Well, you will love the Navy," he countered. "I can see you standing on the bow of a great Navy ship as it slices through the water. In fact," continued the recruiter, "You have the look of a Naval Officer."

I guess that was a compliment.

"Anyway, I do not see you in Vietnam," he continued. "I see you in the Mediterranean."

I was becoming more interested.

"Yes, the Med, and do you know what is special about the Med?" he asked.

I had absolutely no idea. Was the water different? Was there special compensation for being there? I had no idea what was special about the Med.

"WOMEN," shouted the recruiter as his voice became shriller. "Beautiful women from Spain to France to Greece. You will be getting laid every night in port."

Why did it always come back to women? Was I that transparent? By now, he had my full attention. Just sign with us, and you will be on your way to a sex life you will never forget.

I was leaning. The Navy was gaining ground, but I did want to visit the Marines. After all, I owed it to the Major's daughter. Even if I did not get in, I could tell her I tried to enlist, but they had no openings at this time. She might reconsider, and the Navy uniforms were blue, and perhaps in the darkness, she might not know the difference. Besides what the Navy Officer was saying, maybe the Major's daughter would not be so important when compared to the European beauties. With all these thoughts racing through my mind, I told the Navy recruiter I would be back after lunch.

"Not a problem," he said, "We will sign you up at that time."

Upon leaving the Navy recruiter, I walked down the hall to the Marine Recruiting Office and walked in. The reception was slightly different. No one jumped up to meet me. No one welcomed me or even looked at me. Rather, a very serious Marine sitting behind a desk simply glared at me. I wandered over to a table and looked at the literature on the tables. The Marines had firstclass materials, and the colored pictures of Marines in all phases of training, ceremonies, and combat were impressive. No question about it, they knew how to promote themselves. Still, there did not appear to be much interest by the recruiter. He continued to sit at his desk and appeared to be busy. He did not even make eye contact with me. I found this strange and a little unnerving-which was exactly the feeling they were looking for.

I later learned when I worked on Madison Avenue and became savvy in sales, there are different approaches to selling. The most common is to show interest, enthusiasm, a great desire to have you purchase a product or service. Other branches of the military practiced that approach. We want you; we will offer you many good things, we will cover your education, we will give you an adventure, etc. It worked well for them.

The Marines selected another approach. It was called the takeaway. Instead of saying we want you, the Marines said the opposite. We only take the best, and from what we see, you do not measure up. We don't want you. The approach is designed to get a reaction. For many, the reaction is you do not want me, fine, I will go elsewhere. Since the Marines are smaller than the other branches, they did not need as many recruits; therefore, that reaction is OK with them. Go somewhere else, we don't care. What they really wanted was the person who was aggressive, angry, a chip on his shoulder, and perhaps something to prove—the person who would take offense at being rejected. The person who would say-wait a minute, I can be one of you. I'll show you. That was their strategy, and they had perfected it to a science.

Therefore, as I glanced through the material, I was being watched by a Marine, who I later learned was a Gunnery Sergeant with many battle ribbons. But at this time, I had no idea what rank was or what the ribbons represented. All I knew was he did not seem impressed at all with my being there. Finally, with a hard scowl, he spoke. "You think you want to be a Marine Officer?"

"Perhaps," I said. Perhaps it was not the answer he was looking for. "Perhaps," he growled, moving closer to me.

"Well," I stammered, "It looks like fun."

I am not sure why I said that, but the reaction was immediate.

"Fun," he screamed, "FUN!"

By now, his face had turned red, his eyes were filled with rage, and the veins in his neck were throbbing. I thought he was going to explode. I had seen coaches get upset when I played sports, but nothing compared to this moment. I was contemplating the thought that he was going to kill me.

"Let me tell you, college boy, a Marine officer has to make decisions in an instant," he said as he snapped his fingers as if he needed to get more of my attention. "Men's lives depend on that ability," he continued, "And you do not appear to be able to make a decision."

With that, he turned away, stormed back to his desk, and slammed his fist on the desk.

"A waste of our time," he mumbled, just loud enough for me to hear.

Later, I wondered how often he had rehearsed that move. But now, I was stunned and starting to get angry. What does he mean, I cannot make a decision? I had made plenty of decisions-especially in sports. After more thought, I walked to his desk.

"I can make a decision," I said.

That was what they were looking for. Someone who would stand up, express himself, not be beaten down. The sergeant knew he had his man. But the sale was not completed. An officer must swear you in, and there was no way the sergeant would let me leave.

A button was pushed, and quickly a Marine captain stood in front of me. There was no handshake, no welcome, no glad to see you.

"Raise your right hand," commanded the officer.

He did not appear to be happy. Quickly, being sure I had the right one, I slowly raised my right hand. The captain proceeded to issue me the oath of office.

"Do you swear to uphold the laws and defend the constitution," etc., etc. recited the captain.

He stopped. "I do," was my reply.

"Good," said the captain, and he promptly disappeared.

At this point, the sergeant moved forward. I expected him to congratulate me, thank me, welcome me. Not happening.

"Sign this form and put down your address. Your orders will be mailed to you. You will report at the prescribed time to Quantico, Virginia, for Officer Candidate School for training. Maybe you will graduate. Now leave, I am busy."

I walked by the Navy office in a daze, back out the door and into the car where my roommates were waiting. They had saved me a beer, which I gulped down along with part of a grinder.

"Well, did you join up?" said Rick with a grin on his face.

"Yeah," I said, still in shock from my encounter.

"You will like the Air Force," Rick continued.

"I didn't join the Air Force," I replied.

"The Navy is good," chimed in Skip. I think he once had an uncle in the Navy.

"I didn't join the Navy," I replied again.

The car became quiet. It was Jimmy's turn to speak. Jimmy's father had served in the Marines in World War II. Not a desk job but as an infantryman on Okinawa. The costliest battle for the Marines in World War II. More Marines died on Okinawa than even on Iwo Jima. Not many people know that. Jimmy's dad saw a lot of action, and he knew firsthand what war was really like. A far cry from the John Wayne movies. Men died, lots of them. He had discussed those events with his son, and while he was very patriotic and would want his son to defend our country, he had grave doubts about Vietnam. Why were we there, and what was our strategy? Those were questions that men who had seen war tended to ask while others were drawn to the glamor of the uniforms and the marching bands.

"You didn't join the Marines?" said Jimmy.

"Well yes, I did," I said quietly.

"Oh God, Gris," was all Jimmy could say.

We were close, and at that moment I know he feared for his friend and what I was going to do. No one else said anything. Rick drove the car back to the school. We got out and went to class. At that point, I was only sure of one thing. I was going to be a Marine.

**My Roommates
Rick Ives, Skip Smith, and Jim Madore**

Summertime

Preparation

School ended. I graduated and was home for the summer. As decreed, my orders arrived. I had one month to get ready.

The reaction to my decision was met with a wide range of emotions. My poor mother was heartbroken. I was her only son, and the Vietnam casualty figures were mounting. As usual, the Marines had more deaths than the other branches of the services, although the Army was gaining ground. She supported my choice, but it was hard on her. My relatives were surprised. I am sure most thought I would never get through the training. Their lack of confidence in my future was not too encouraging. On the other hand, the Major was impressed. More drinks were ordered, and he supplied more stories of Marine conquests.

"You have made the best decision of your life," he said. "One thing, though, you must get in shape. Run every day and do sit-ups and pull-ups. Your training will not be easy. I promise you that."

I agreed to follow his advice and set a strict exercise regimen for myself.

Of course, most important to me was the response of his daughter.

"I am going to be a Marine," I told her with great pride.

"You haven't made it yet," was her coy reply.

Lord, she could tease, which of course, only inflamed my desperate desires. She would allow a certain amount of activity, but there would be no home runs. You had to have those dress blues for a home run.

So, in the summer of '66, I began my workouts. Just like in the movie *Rocky*, I would get up each morning and start to run. There was a hill near where I lived called Johnny Cake Hill, and I would run up the hill, veer off into the woods and run up and down an old trail. It was at least two miles. Then I would run back-around four miles in all. At first, I could not do it without stopping at least five times. But it became easier as time went on. I did 30 pushups and went to the high school gym, where I did seven pullups and climbed ropes, which I knew would be expected in Marine training.

During the day, I worked as a lifeguard at the local beach club. It was my first real job, and I reported directly to a colonel who had served in the British Army. As manager of club operations, he schooled me in proper maintenance procedures and attention to detail. Each morning, I would meet the colonel at the front door of the club at precisely ten o'clock. The colonel would be dressed in a khaki shirt, khaki shorts, and knee high white socks. He wore a white pith helmet and carried a swagger stick. Swagger sticks were short sticks that resembled the baton a musical conductor might employ to lead an orchestra. They were popular in the British Army, and the colonel fit the role, looking as if he just stepped out of a Rudyard Kipling novel.

I would say: "Good morning Colonel Smith," and he would answer,

"Good morning David, follow me," and the inspection was on. He would inspect the main building for cleanliness and then walk out the front door and turn right to the upper deck. I had set out the tables, chairs, and umbrellas, and alignment, and spacing was critical. The swagger stick would serve as a ruler to ensure proper spacing. At times, he would reach into his pocket and put on a white glove to run over the tables. The glove needed to remain white.

Upon inspection of the decks, the colonel turned to the beach. He took great pride in the condition of the sand and basked in the positive comments he received from the membership. The beach was raked every day with large hay rakes. Only shells and pebbles small enough to pass between the teeth of the rake would be permitted to remain under no conditions would there be any seaweed. The beach would be raked north to south one day and east to west the next. Of great importance to the colonel were the rows left by the rake. They had to be straight. Wavy rows were an indication of a lack of focus and good order. On more than one occasion, I would be required to rerake the beach under his stern glare.

Following the beach, we would go to the end of the pier. There were ropes for railings and turnbuckles at each end to adjust them. The colonel would tap the ropes with the swagger stick to ensure proper tension, and I would adjust the turnbuckles as required. Next, the colonel would produce binoculars from the lifeguard stand. He would scan the waters for seaweed, floating logs, or jellyfish. If spotted, I would be required to get in the boat tied to the pier and capture the offending object. Then the colonel would survey the raft. It had to be spotless. Cleaning equipment was in the boat, and the raft would be scrubbed multiple times in a day if necessary. I developed a real hatred of seagulls.

The inspections took around forty minutes, and then a debriefing was held along with instructions for the remainder of the day. Room for improvement was the most common comment, but I did receive an occasional well done. It was quite an entree into the world of work and great preparation for what lay ahead. After the inspection and any needed corrections, I would spend the rest of the day swimming, watching girls, and working on my tan.

As August approached, my training was paying off. I could now run the five miles without stopping, and my time was considerably faster. Pull-ups were up to ten, and sit-ups were at 100. I was in good shape and ready for anything the Marines could throw at me. That would be a slight miscalculation.

Officer Candidate School

The day of reckoning arrived. I was off to Quantico, Virginia. I was told to bring nothing but the clothes on my back. That was easy. I boarded the train in Connecticut and headed to Washington, DC. After a brief stop, the train rolled south across the Potomac and followed the coast. After a few more stops, the train arrived in the small town of Quantico, Virginia. It was around four o'clock—1600 as I was to learn. A young Marine asked if I was there to go to training, I said I was.

"Over here," he said.

He seemed friendly enough. Not what I was prepared for. There was a trailer with seats inside. The Marines called them cattle cars. I climbed aboard and sat down. There were a few other college-aged men on the bus or cattle cars. We talked quietly.

"No talking,'" said the Marine.

We sat there. As time went on, more men climbed aboard. We continued to sit. It was hot, sweat dripped off us. Four o'clock became five, and then six. More men joined our group. Finally, the young Marine climbed into the driver's seat, and the bus pulled away from the station. No yelling, no orders, just a quiet bus ride. So far, so good. We rode out of the town and passed the gate that read *Quantico, Crossroads of the Marine Corps*. We passed office buildings and here and there saw Marines walking by. We progressed into more open areas and finally to a camp surrounded by woods. Here there were more Marines. We were told to get off the bus and go into an office. Inside lined with tables, we shuffled along, repeating our names and addresses as Marines checked us off lists. The process took 20 minutes. When we were all together, there must have been around 40 of us, we were told to go outside. By now, it was dark, and we walked into a courtyard between two large brick buildings. Suddenly, out of nowhere, he appeared flanked by two other Marines.

Staff Sergeant (SSGT) Vic

He was around 5' 11," and I would guess about 180 pounds. He had a square jaw and broad shoulders. But what was most distinguishing was his scowling face and his voice. His voice was like a foghorn. Deep and loud. He was able to project as if he had a loudspeaker. It was clear, concise, and commanding. He was Staff Sergeant Vic, and he was our senior drill instructor.

"Line up in three columns, tallest to shortest, no talking, you have one minute to get this done," growled SSgt Vic.

We stumbled around in the dark, trying to follow his command. I was not sure what a column was. The other two sergeants moved among us, pushing and moving us around to fit into the formations that were called. As it turned out, these would become the squads that would form up the platoon, but at that moment, all I knew was I was in the first column, the second man. To my right was the tallest member of the platoon. His name was Kel, and he was a basketball star from Alabama. We became lifelong friends. To my left was Troy, one of the most squared away members of the platoon. Being in the first squad put you in the direct eye of SSgt Vic. This was not necessarily a good thing.

After we had lined up, SSgt Vic began to speak. First on the agenda was standing at attention. As I was to quickly learn, nothing in the Marine Corps was designed to be easy. The smallest detail was critically important. The Marine philosophy was to take care of the small things, and the large problems will fall into place. This belief system had served them well in their glorious history. Certainly, no college kids were going to change that opinion. Do exactly as we say, or you are gone, was their creed. The notion that anyone can join the service did not apply to the Marines and certainly not to Marine Corps Officers.

Standing at attention, your forefinger and thumb must be together, the rest of your fingers were cupped in a row. The thumb and forefinger were on your trouser seams, your shoulders back, stomach in, head and eyes straight.

"I want to see an equal amount of white on each side of your eyeballs," growled SSgt Vic. The two other sergeants moved among us, correcting the slightest deviation from this command. It must have been 15 minutes before SSgt Vic was satisfied that we had some semblance of military bearing. Then he began.

"You candidates," we were candidates to become Marines. We were not yet Marines.

"You candidates had choices," he barked. "You could have gone to other services; they probably would have taken you. You chose us. Understand, we did not choose you. You do exactly as we say, you have an opportunity to lead Marines, fail to do so, and you will not. It's that simple."

"Now, you will be housed on the second floor of Building A, which is to your right. When I tell you, you will get upstairs in Building A. First column will be bunks on the right, the second column bunks farther down on the right and up on the left, and third column remaining bunks on the left. I want to see you in the exact positions you are now. You have exactly five minutes to get this done. Dismissed."

With that, we all scrambled upstairs to our barracks. It was total chaos. Men bumped into one another, trying to decide who would have the upper or lower bunk. There was confusion as to where one squad ended, and another started. I was with Kel, and we took the first bunk since we were one and two in the first squad. I chose the top, and he agreed. We were ahead of many who were still trying to figure what bunk was there's and who would be on the upper or lower.

The two sergeants stood back watching. Little did we know we were being tested from day one. Did you try, did you work together, did you help one another to figure things out. If you did not participate or help one another, you were immediately targeted as someone to watch. The weeding out process had begun. After the two sergeants had gotten us into some semblance of order, SSgt Vic reappeared.

"You will find a towel on the bunks. Take off all your clothes, wrap the towel around you, then hit the head (Bathroom-the Marines used Navy terminology since they served on ships) and get back here, stand at attention, and try to remember what I told you."

Clothes off, towels around us, we poured into the head and then reassembled back at our bunks, trying to stand at attention with our towels wrapped around us. Not knowing what was coming next, we were scared; plus, we were tired. I'd left Connecticut early in the morning, and it was now close to ten o'clock at night. As the drill instructors were slowly walking down the three rows of candidates, the unthinkable happened. It seems in my haste to comply with orders, I had done a poor job of tying the knot on my towel. As SSgt Vic moved closer, the knot slipped, and my stupid towel fell to the floor. What could I do? I did not dare break from attention, and so I had no choice but to remain standing there stark naked. Fear produces an immediate reaction to parts of the male anatomy. I was humiliated. God, if the Major's daughter could see me now, she would be greatly disappointed. SSgt Vic passed by me and just shook his head. I could not have felt worse if he'd punched me in the face.

Drilling

After the humiliating disaster of the first night, I began to slowly get into the swing of things. We were under time constraints to do everything from the simplest tasks to the more complicated. But nowhere were things more intense than on the drill field. We marched every day for hours. I can still hear SSgt Vic barking out:

"Three to the front, six to the rear."

That meant swung your hands three inches forward, six inches back.

"Stop bouncing."

Meaning you marched from the waist down.

"Heels, heels, heels."

Meaning you jammed your heels down first.

"Left face, right face, about-face, to the rear march" over and over and over.

Most impressive was his ability to call out the cadence. It is hard to describe, but it had a rhythm to it, and you went by sounds more than actual words. Each sergeant had perfected their own ways of calling cadence. Each was different, and you learned to differentiate one voice from another. SSgt Vic's was hard not to miss. There was no question our platoon was one of the best because of his style and professionalism.

Then we graduated from just marching to drilling with rifles. We had been issued rifles-M-14's, and we would march to the drill field to practice the manual of arms-rifle movements. There was one exception. One candidate had been told that Quantico had an exceptional golf course. Therefore, he had arrived for training with his golf clubs on his shoulder.

"Where is the golf course?" he asked one of the sergeants.

So, for the first week, he drilled with his golf clubs.

"Get me, Arnold Palmer," screamed SSgt Vic.

It was pretty funny in retrospect.

The drilling continued—hour after hour in the hot Virginia sun. We would drill on a large concrete slab known as the grinder, learning the rifle movements-port arms, right shoulder arms, left shoulder arms. Day after day, week after week, we drilled. At first, our drilling was sloppy, but as time progressed, we became more and more precise. Soon a command produced a single sound of hands slapping against the wooden stocks of the rifles. We were good. From 40 raw recruits who had little or no military experience, the Marines were transforming us into a team that functioned as one. With that came discipline, concentration, attention to detail, and, most important, pride. To a man, we felt we were special. Exactly as planned.

The Rifle Range

If drilling, physical fitness, running, marching, and lectures were important-and, they were- it all paled compared to the rifle range. All Marines are first and foremost riflemen. You had to qualify on the rifle range, or you were out. No exceptions. To qualify, you had to be able to achieve an acceptable score standing at 200 yards, kneeling at 300 yards and prone at 500 yards. 500 hundred yards is five football fields. At that range, the bull's eye on the targets looked like quarters.

As usual, I figured this would be easy. After all, I had hunted ducks around my family properties, and hitting a duck as it flew by was a challenge. Of course, I was firing a shotgun, which allows for more mistakes than a single-shot rifle; but no matter. I would excel in this part of training. Once again, a miscalculation.

As with everything else, the Marines' attention to detail was evident. Strapping in so the rifle would not drift, spot wells where you positioned your cheek, the pull on your trigger finger, the adjustments to the wind, known as Kentucky windage, all had to be mastered. Convinced, I knew it all, I did not apply the level of attention that was required. As a result, on our first day, I failed to qualify. This was serious, and I was scared. Those who did not qualify were sent to classes where we were schooled on how to do things correctly. The sergeants were relentless in their demands. Their instruction was by the numbers and repetition. Repeat the process over and over. My arm was black and blue from the straps, and my shoulder ached from the constant recoil of the rifle. But I learned.

In the Marine Corps, there are three levels of accomplishment on the rifle range. The absolute best shooters are experts, and very few can achieve that level, maybe 20%. The second is a sharpshooter, and that is very good. Maybe 40%. Last is a marksman, which is average. There is nothing below that. If you do not qualify, you are gone. When we completed a week of the range, we would receive our shooting badges. Experts got medals shaped in an oak leaf cluster around rifles, sharpshooters got crossed rifles, and marksman got a target which was sarcastically referred to as a toilet seat. I shot sharp-shooter and was proud of the accomplishment. Shortly after that, the same training was applied to the 45-caliber pistol. Again, I shot sharpshooter.

Pugil Sticks

Pugil Sticks are unique to the Maine Corps. Designed to develop bayonet skills; they are small poles with large canvas bags on each end—kind of a giant Q-tip. The idea is two combatants protected by football helmets, and a large protective cup enter a circle and use bayonet skills to score points on the other Marines. In reality, it is an opportunity for each Marine to try and destroy his opponent. It promotes an extremely aggressive attitude in Marines.

We lined up in a column of twos and went at it. The Sergeants would yell motivational messages about your family, sister, whatever, and the idea was to promote rage and a better fight. The first two potential officers did not quite get the idea. They sparred and tried to score points with plenty of feints and missed jabs. The sergeants went nuts. Screaming and shouting profanities, they wanted fighters, not dancers!

It was now my turn. I was paired up with John from DC in great shape with a rock hard body. We ventured into the pit, and I led with a somewhat soft jab. John answered by hitting me in the side of the head with a hard-left thrust. I staggered and fell backward. His sergeant was delighted and screamed for the kill. My sergeant was furious and threatened to beat me worse than my attacker. Urged on, John hit me again and moved in for the victory. My head was throbbing, and I was in trouble. At this point, I forgot about the training and fell back on my baseball skills. I rose to one knee, slid my hands all the way to the end of the stick, and swung as hard as I could. I caught him in the stomach and knocked the wind out of him. Straggling to my feet, we were both hurting. After a few more swings at each other, the whistle blew. It was deemed a draw.

"That's more like it," was SSgt Vic's response.

I had survived a match up with a very tough opponent.

My next opponent was quite different. Charlie was his name, and he had graduated from Harvard. Obviously, he was very smart and a nice guy as well. Charlie was well-liked in the platoon. The sergeants recognized his intelligence and were not quite as hard on him. Yet, we were Marines, and we had to fight. The usual harassment was forthcoming as we entered the pit for another pugil stick battle.

As the fight began, I was stronger, quicker, and a better athlete. But Charlie was tall and blessed with long arms. Not wanting to get hit, Charlie twisted his arms back and forth like a windmill. Try as I might, I could not get close. He kept moving those long arms, and while he did not hurt me, I could not score any points. It was like trying to penetrate a fan. My sergeant was screaming at me to attack, and Charlie's sergeant was laughing at my futile efforts. It was humiliating. Finally, the whistle blew, and Charlie was declared the winner by default, as I had done nothing. I was furious and slammed my helmet to the ground amidst more cursing from my sergeant. Then there was a hand on my shoulder. It was from Charlie.

"Hey," he said. "Don't feel badly-you were much better. I was just lucky being able to hold you off."

"Yeah," I mumbled and walked off. I was so mad I couldn't even acknowledge the kindness Charlie had shown. Looking back, I wish I had.

Three months later, Charlie stepped off a helicopter in Dong Ho, and a piece of shrapnel from an enemy artillery round ricocheted off a steel box, hit him in the carotid artery, and killed him instantly. To this day, I regret not having been nicer to him. He certainly didn't have to befriend me at that time. He could have basked in the glory of beating me. But instead, he reached out, and all I did was walk away.

Years later, I stood in the Chapel at Harvard and saw his name on a list of those who had been killed in the war. I immediately thought of our pugil stick fight and how I wish I could have thanked him. If there was a lesson to be learned, I think it would be to appreciate those who do nice things and thank them. I have tried to remember that lesson in dealing with people, but I still wish I could have learned from a different experience.

Bernie's Boys

After five weeks of intense training, SSgt Vic announced we had two days off. We could go off base; Washington DC was the destination of most. SSgt Vic's only restriction was we could not go into the bars of Quantico because that is where he drank.

In the town of Quantico was the Sportsman Lounge owned by Mr. Bernie Terreny and operated by his three sons. Mr. Terrney was a personal friend of Kel's father, who was a Marine Lieutenant Colonel. Kel and I had become close friends. Even though we were not supposed to go into Quantico, the fact that Kel knew the owner of the bar was exciting and would probably result in some free beers. Which it did.

Mr. Terrney welcomed Kel and me to his restaurant. On this particular night, Mr. Terreny was shorthanded. Two of his boys were out, and there was no one to handle the bar.

"No problem," said Kel. "Gris and I will take over."

Pouring beers was fun, and we were having a great time when in walked SSgt Vic and three other sergeants.

"Aren't these your candidates?" one said to SSgt Vic.

SSgt Vic stared in disbelief. Not only had we gone into the bars against his orders but were about to serve him beers. Kel took the orders, and I poured the beers. SSgt Vic drank his beer, said nothing, and rapidly departed. I wondered if he would forget the incident.

The next day, we had completed more physical training, and the platoon was tired and ready to turn in for the night. Suddenly, SSgt Vic appeared.

"Get me Bernie's Boys," he commanded.

Kel and I stepped forward and were taken to the edge of the squad bay (building), where we were given two shovels.

"The Lieutenant wants a trench-two-foot-deep all around the building. Get busy."

Two hours later, we had dug the trench. Then the Lieutenant appeared.

"What are you doing," he demanded? "Get this filled in immediately."

Captain Paul H. Kellogg Jr
a.k.a Kel

Not wanting to argue with the Lieutenant, we took another half hour to fill in the trench. By now, we could hardly stand up. In a scene right out of the movie, *Cool Hand Luke,* where the prison guards make the prisoner, played by Paul Neman, repeat digging, SSgt Vic appeared and demanded to know where his trench was.

"The Lieutenant told us to fill it in," I offered.

"I do not see any Lieutenant; you must be hallucinating. Dig the trench."

So, under the Virginia moon, Kel and I redug the trench. In all, it was over four hours of digging, and I vowed never to go into another bar. Obviously, I was delirious.

Weeding Out

As we progressed in training, it was apparent that not everyone was cut out to lead Marines. Physical fitness was one disqualifier. I remain grateful to the Major, not only for his beautiful daughter but for telling me to get in shape. You had to do at least six pullups. By now, I was up to 12. A rather heavyset man not far from my bunk was hard-pressed to do four. One day his bunk was stripped, empty. That is how it worked. One by one bunks would be emptied. Another critical area was the ability to react under stress and solve problems in a given timeframe. One of the sergeant's favorite tricks was to take all the bedding in the barracks and throw it into the center of the squad bay.

"You people have 10 minutes to get this straightened out and your bunks back in order," screamed the sergeants.

Back in order meant they could bounce quarters off your bunks. That was impossible to accomplish in 10 minutes, and they knew it. But they watched. Along with the ways one or two would say things like this is stupid, it can't be done, to hell with it. Those statements and attitudes produced more empty bunks. An officer in combat can never give up, no matter what the circumstances. The rifle range got a few more. Then there were peer evaluations where you rated each other from the top five to the bottom five. You were in serious trouble if you were in the bottom five. That meant that your peers did not think you were fit to lead Marines. The sergeants put stock in the evaluations. But of all the empty bunks, one stood out.

One of our candidates, let's call him Ed, bragged to everyone that his girlfriend was in the Miss America contest. I am not sure if it was at the national or state level, but it was still a connection to fame that anyone would be proud to share. It was not the accomplishment, but the way this candidate went about telling everyone about it that caused problems. He came across that he was special, superior, better than everyone else. I am special because my girlfriend is beautiful. One thing SSgt Vic despised was individuals. We were a team. No one was better than anyone else. We functioned and succeed as a team. Anyone who thought they were better than anyone else interfered with that message. With that in mind, SSgt Vic and the other sergeants were watching, waiting. Ed was strong and excelled in physical fitness, drilling, the rifle range, and had the bearing to make a good officer. But this idea that he was better by way of his girlfriend did not make him too popular with us, and it brought out hatred in the Sergeants. They wanted him gone, and they picked their moment.

We were on a three-mile march through the hills. It was late in the day, and we were tired, tempers were short, and the constant yelling and screaming were playing on everyone's nerves. To make matters worse, it was raining, and the mud was slippery. Men fell, got up, and continued to run covered in mud. Keep in mind we were running with forty-pound packs, rifles, and a cartridge belt loaded down with two canteens, a first aid kit, four magazines of ammunition, and a bayonet. Add mud and rain to this list, and it was hard. No one was happy. It was the perfect time to nail Ed. One of the sergeants moved up to him and said,

"You know, the only reason girls get into the Miss America contest is they (blank) the judges."

That was all it took. Ed exploded and pushed the sergeant. What happened next was a blur. Four sergeants, including a 6'5" monster from another platoon, surrounded him. Putting your hands on a drill instructor was unheard of, unthinkable. Ed was gone in an instant. He may have been vaporized. I have no idea. All I know was when we returned to the barracks, his bunk was empty.

In all, we lost over 20% of our original candidates.

The House Mouse

Our training was intense. Every day we were told this procedure, or this weapon or this strategy is necessary to keep you and your men alive. We were up by 5:30 AM and hit the racks (bed) by 10:00 PM. In between, there was constant motion. Never did we just stand around. We simply went from one activity to another. With this type of pressure, you needed some relief-some levity. SSgt Vic had led many training units, and he knew this was important.

Enter the House Mouse. The house mouse was a candidate selected by SSgt Vic, who would do errands and get SSgt Vic and the other sergeants' items for the day. The person SSgt Vic selected was a kid from New York City. He was perfect for the job. First, he was well-liked and had the personality to handle the tasks. Second, he had a highpitched voice that resembled Barney Fife, the bumbling deputy on *The Andy Griffith Show,* and it added a sense of levity. But third and perhaps most important, he was somewhat of a celebrity. But unlike Ed, who bragged about his Miss America girlfriend, he never spoke unless asked about his claim to fame. The fame was that he and a few of his college friends had formed a band called *The Fireballs*, and they had recorded a song. Our candidate was the drummer, and the song had become a big hit. In fact, it was in the top five on the billboard, and he and the Fireballs had appeared on the Dick Clark Show. We were impressed. So perhaps to make sure he did not get a big head, SSgt Vic had selected him to be the House Mouse

"House Mouse," yelled SSgt Vic, "Get me some paper and a pen."

The House Mouse would answer, "Yes, Platoon Sergeant," and run off to accomplish the request.

The one event that would highlight the adventures of the House Mouse occurred during the eighth week of training. By now, we were in step with the procedures—those who had difficultly adjusting had either shaped up or shipped out. What remained was a group of young men who were getting close to graduation and becoming Marine Officers. It was a Saturday morning around 11, and we were putting the finishing touches on cleaning the squad bay, polishing our equipment, and pressing our uniforms. If we passed inspections, we would have the afternoon off. Everyone had become skilled at these assignments, and we were confident we would pass. SSgt Vic had entered the Squad bay and was preparing for the inspection. He was joined that morning by Sgt Johnson. Sgt Johnson was the junior platoon instructor and did not say too much. He did not have to. He was a large Marine from Mississippi whose main job was to assist and enforce anything SSgt Vic said. With his size and scowling face, he accomplished his mission without much effort. Nobody questioned Sgt Johnson.

SSgt Vic glanced out the window as he was preparing to begin the inspection. Suddenly he stopped dead in his tracks and stared out the window.

"What have we here," he growled in a deep voice. Sgt Johnson joined him, and he too stared out the window.

"Never seen anything like it," said Sgt Johnson.

"How the hell did they get on the base?" SSgt Vic exclaimed.

By now, all of us were beginning to move towards the window. What had caught SSgt Vic's eyes was a Volkswagen bus from the hippie era. It was painted multi colors-reds, yellows, blues, and greens, with peace signs and make love, not war slogans. The two sergeants were stunned. At that moment, it got worse. The door of the van opened and out stepped three long haired men. At least we thought they were men, but it was kind of hard to tell. They had many colored clothes that were completely mismatched, ill fitting, and nothing was coordinated. One had a big floppy hat, and one had on granny glasses like the ones John Lennon wore. They were slumped over and appeared to be hanging out. The comparison between our two sergeants and these three could not have been more obvious. Both sergeants had black spitshined shoes that looked like mirrors, their trousers were perfectly cut, and you could cut paper on the creases. Their belts were bleached white, and the belt buckles were shined to the point that would blind you if the sun hit them just so. Their shirts fit perfectly on flat stomachs and broad shoulders. Numerous colored battle ribbons were pinned in rows over their left breast pocket. Their hair was cut high and tight, and their caps with the Marine Corps emblem were positioned exactly two fingers above their nose. Comparing this description to the three hippies was comical.

As the two sergeants continued to stare out the window, there was a knock on the wall. It was the corporal of the guard.

"SSgt Vic," called the corporal.

"What do you want, Corporal?" asked SSgt Vic.

"These men say they want to see their drummer," said the Corporal, who was extremely nervous in front of SSgt Vic.

"What," screamed SSgt Vic. "They want our House-Mouse?"

Kel elbowed me, "Gris, this is going to be classic."

I smiled.

"House Mouse, front and center," bellowed SSgt Vic.

"Yes, platoon sergeant," said the House Mouse with the Barney Fife voice.

"What the hell is this-who are these long hair hippie freaks?"

The House Mouse looked out the window.

"They are my band the fire-" he did not finish the word.

"The what?" growled SSgt Vic. "The fireplugs, the firemen, the fire eaters, listen House Mouse, are you trying to destroy my Marine Corps with these characters that resemble an explosion in a Goodwill store?"

The House Mouse started to stammer in his high pitched voice, "I guess they just want- "

"You guess."

"Well," stammered the poor House Mouse.

"Sgt Johnson," commanded SSgt Vic,

"Alert the Base Commander, we have subversives on the base."

By this time, we were all laughing, and SSgt Vic was playing this to the hilt.

"Are you working for the Viet Cong?" demanded SSgt Vic.

"He might be," added Sgt Johnson as he moved forward in a threatening manner.

The poor House Mouse was not sure what was going to happen next.

"Listen, House Mouse," continued SSgt Vic, "You get down there and tell those long haired hippies, freak, communist loving, Viet Cong degenerates they have exactly five minutes to get off this base, or I will have them shot."

The House Mouse was near panic. Without hesitation, he ran downstairs and screamed to his band:

"Get out, get out, or you will be shot."

The Fireballs, who had driven all the way down to Virginia from New York City to visit their drummer on a beautiful Saturday morning, leaped back in their van and were gone. The platoon was laughing so hard, we had tears in our eyes. SSgt Vic just smiled.

The Basic School

Time passed, and those of us fortunate enough to graduate from Officer Candidate School were now Marines. A graduation was held in a large auditorium, and various officers spoke of the pride of the Marine Corps and how we would be expected to carry on the tradition. At the end of the ceremony, the band played the Marine Corps Hymn, and it was the proudest moment of my life. I had achieved the title of Marine Corps Officer without any family connections or sliding through by charming someone. I had earned that title with hard work and a determination to never quit, no matter the circumstances. For the first time in my life, I felt like a success. I had more or less failed in school. Certainly, I did not achieve at any level close to my family's accomplishments. Athletically, I had played varsity sports, but not at the level of my father. Socially, I had enjoyed the company of several women, but I was not close to marriage. By all accounts, I had fallen short of expectations. But this was different. I had managed to achieve recognition and success on my own.

My mother drove down from Connecticut for the ceremony, and she pinned my Second Lieutenant bars on my shoulder. She had watched over me during my teenage years and had seen to it that I had received a good education. I owed her everything. I just wished my father had been there, but I felt his spirit with me.

Proud as we were, there was no liberty to enjoy our accomplishment. The Vietnam War was in full swing, and we were needed. We would be sent to The Basic School for three more months of training. The Basic School was more like college. We were housed in dormitories, three to a room. There was a little less pressure on the physical side and a great deal more on the academic side. There was more to becoming an officer than running up and down hills and drilling with a rifle.

Under the direction of a seasoned Marine Corps captain, we were exposed to every weapon the Marines had, from grenade launchers and machine guns to tanks, artillery, Marine aircraft, and Naval gunfire. We had to know how they operated and how to employ them in a wide variety of circumstances. It was serious with the instructors constantly saying what I am going to tell you will be vital to keeping you and your men alive in combat. It was never lost on us that in just a few months, we would be fighting in Vietnam.

Most important of all, the instruction was tactical deployments. How to move and position squads, platoons, and companies in combat situations. Every officer must know tactics, and they better excel at it. Other services left that to the infantry, but the Marines believed that whether you were in engineers, artillery, tanks, communications, supply, or motor transport, there could come a day when you would have to fight. At that time, you better be able to lead Marines in combat. It had served them well in other wars, as it would in this one. It certainly was for me.

Then there were other aspects of being an officer and caring for your men. Lessons on safety, first-aid, sanitation, legal requirements, and uniforms. Marine history that outlined not only the proud accomplishment of the Corps but how they achieved those results often against superior numbers. Again, no detail was too small. Tests were given, and we were graded.

Based on those grades and to some extent on your preferences, you could select your military occupational specialty (MOS). While I had done very well in the physical aspects of training, my struggles in the classroom would eliminate me from the infantry, artillery, and air. I chose transportation that included trucks and amphibious tractors, which were the vehicles that Marines used to assault beaches. I would provide security and lead convoys to resupply troops utilizing these machines. With that decision, I graduated from The Basic School in March of 1967. I had been at Quantico for eight months, and it was time for a new assignment. That would be Camp Lejeune, North Carolina.

Gearing Up

Camp Lejeune

Camp Lejeune is the largest Marine Corps base on the east coast. It encompasses 246 square miles on the coast of North Carolina. It has numerous rivers and bays, which makes it ideal for amphibious training. In fact, it is the largest amphibious training base in the world.

While going through the training of how to run convoys and deploy security teams, I was assigned to a company to learn firsthand the way things worked. This would be my first exposure to the troops, and I was happy to show everyone what I had learned. This was a typical reaction from a brand-new Second Lieutenant. That is when I met Sergeant Tom.

Sergeant Tom had been in the Marine Corps forever. He should have been a Sergeant Major by now, but Sergeant Tom had a drinking issue. It caused him to be busted on many occasions. Despite his love of whiskey, Sergeant Tom really knew tactics, equipment, and, most importantly, how to deal with troops. He had been in the Chosen Reservoir in Korea when the Marines were surrounded by over 100,000 enemies. Faced with almost certain death and 30 degrees below zero weather, the Marines had fought their way out in one of the greatest battles in the history of modern warfare. Anyone who survived the "Frozen Chosen" deserved a few drinks. He had the words "Chosen Few" tattooed on his arm and was revered by the men. I liked him immediately.

Quick to show everyone how committed I was to be leading a platoon, I started running around telling everyone what to do. The troops complied with a *Here we go again with a new Lieutenant* attitude. Sergeant Tom stood off in the distance, watching. He had seen this before. Finally, he had seen enough.

"May I have a word with the Lieutenant?" he asked.

Then Sergeant Tom gave me the best advice I was to hear in the Marines.

"If the Lieutenant would like Sir, let me tell you how this works. You tell me what you want to be done, and it will get done. However, if you want to do my job, I'll be at the club. Let me know how it works out."

I got the message.

The three months passed rapidly, and I was given 30 days off before deploying to Vietnam. During that time, I had learned a great deal, thanks mostly to Sergeant Tom. One night over much alcohol, Sergeant Tom paid me one of the best compliments of my life.

"Lieutenant, you have real leadership ability, it just seems to come naturally to you. The troops will follow you. Remember to work with your senior sergeants, and together you will do great things. I expect you to kick ass in the Nam."

I thanked him for everything. He was old Corps and had his problems, but he was a true Marine and a hero from the Chosen. I was privileged and fortunate to meet him.

Massacre on the Boardwalk

Along with Kel, another friendship for me was with a stocky Marine from Ohio. His name was Mike, but because of his size, he was known as "Bear." He had played sports in college and had excelled in pugil stick fighting back at Officer Candidate School. While he could fight, he was very friendly and loved to kid around. That plus his love of sports brought us together.

One day with less than a week to go before leaving Camp Lejeune, Mike AKA the Bear, and I decided we would have some well-earned rest by traveling to Wrightsville Beach on the North Carolina coast. It was a beautiful sunny day, and we enjoyed the sun, surf, and a few beers. As the day was ending, we walked down the boardwalk where carnival tents and games of chance beckoned. One of particular interest was a shooting range, where for the correct score, you could win large teddy bears hanging from the tent. For Marines highly trained in firing rifles, this would be easy. The carnival barker was a short, fat, bald individual who resembled George Costanza, Jerry Seinfeld's friend from the *Seinfeld* show. He encouraged us with the words,

"You Marines should not have any trouble."

But we did. The sights were broken on the rifles, and I believe the barrels were slightly bent. We could not hit the targets, and the barker was really giving it to us.

"I thought Marines were good shots, you guys are terrible. You couldn't hit water if you fell out of a boat."

We were not amused, and it was getting embarrassing as a crowd was gathering. The heckling continued.

"What do we have to do to win a bear?" asked Mike.

"Forget it, you guys couldn't hit anything," laughed the barker. With that, Mike had had enough.

"I bet I can hit those bears," and with one swing of his large hand, he snapped the chain that held the rifles to the counter. He then swung his rifle up and proceeded to shoot the bears. I thought this was a great idea and joined in. Together we shot up 15 bears. We shot off their heads and arms while the stuffing was flying out of their bodies. It was total carnage with limp bears hanging off their hooks. The George Costanza barker was screaming

"What are you doing? Are you crazy, someone call the police. You are destroying my bears!"

**Captain Michael Hemmert
a.k.a. Bear**

Realizing that local law enforcement could be on their way, we put down the rifles and ran down the boardwalk. We escaped in our car and drove back to camp. We chalked the adventure up to honing our skills to take on the Cong!

30 Days Off

It had been almost a year since I had taken that train to Quantico. Now I was headed home as a well-trained Marine Officer. I was in great shape. I could run those four miles around my home without breaking a sweat. I could do 15 pull-ups and over 200 sit-ups. I had added 10 pounds of upper body muscle. My dress blues were a 42 jacket and pants were a 30-inch waist. They had been individually designed by tailors and fit like a glove.

My mother was proud, although she dreaded my next assignment. A deeply religious woman, she put my life in God's hands. She committed herself to the fun and enjoyment of the next thirty days. For the first time, my relatives were impressed. Most were astounded I had made it, but nevertheless, they were reserved and polite in complimenting me. This was particularly true of the men. Many had served in the Navy, and there is an interesting dynamic between the two branches of the service. While there is good-natured kidding and sometimes fights at the enlisted levels, in truth, both respected each other. The Marines appreciate the ships that take them places, the Naval gunfire, and perhaps, most of all, the Navy pilots flying off carriers in all types of weather to bring them vital air support. In return, the Navy respects the combat assignments. It acknowledges the more rigorous training with the exception perhaps of Navy Seal training. In any event, my Navy relatives were impressed to have a Marine Officer in the family. While all would acknowledge it wasn't Yale, it was worthy of respect.

The Major was thrilled. He looked upon me as his protégé and took credit for my getting through the training. In fairness, he did give me great advice. But my main motivation was standing nearby, in a short skirt and tight sweater. She had never looked better.

"You look good in those dress blues," she smiled.
That line was delivered with the most seductive grin I had ever seen. My blood pressure must have gone up thirty points as my heart pumped enormous amounts of blood into all parts of my body. I swear if I wasn't in such good shape, I would have passed out.

The next thirty days was a grand and glorious time. The major's daughter was one of those women who could look good in anything. In prom type formals, to cocktail dresses, to casual wear, and jeans; she always looked great. And then there were the bathing suits. I was having a wonderful time and gave little thought to what was about to happen. Just enjoy the moment.

Second Lieutenant
David H.W. Griswold

My thirty-day leave passed quickly, and I was down to my last few days before reporting to Nam. Suddenly the realization of the situation took hold. What would happen if I did not return? I recall having been told by our Marine instructors to get our personal affairs in order.

"Some of you will not be coming home," was their constant reminder.

My concern was for my mother. I wanted to spare her as much anguish as possible. With that in mind, I got serious.

I went to the family lawyer and made out a simple will. Everything would go to my mother. I did not have much, but there would be a $24,000 life insurance policy from the military if I was killed. Then there was my major possession-my car. It was the best car I ever had; then or since. It was a 1963 Chevrolet Impala Super Sport convertible. It was a great improvement over my first car. It was candy apple red with a black interior: bucket seats, a beautiful console, and lots of chrome. The wheels sparkled with hubs that had bright red SS's in the center for SuperSport. I loved that car. I had taken it to Florida during my senior year in college for student teaching. A wonderful three months with my college roommates. Riding around on the beaches was the best time of my college life, and we had great times. I suppose I could have put it in a garage for a year and then picked it up upon return. But if I did not return, it would be another terrible task for my poor mother; I elected to sell it to a local car dealer.

I walked into the dealership and told him to give me a fair amount for the car. He said, of course, as a slight smile crossed his face. I signed over the title, gave him the keys, and took his check. I did not even look at it; I was so depressed. I just put the check in my pocket and walked out. I took one last look at this beautiful car that I had polished and waxed to always shine. I walked over and touched it as if to say thank you for all the memories. Then I turned and walked away. As I rode home in silence with a friend who had followed me to the dealer, my sadness was far more than just the car. It was a realization that I was closing the door on the bright college years, all the summer fun, and about to enter a totally different world. The Marines were deadly serious about their training and even more so about combat. Life as I knew it was about to change.

The next day was different. I had been a Red Sox fan since I was a little boy, and in 1967, led by Carl Yastrzemski's triple crown year, the Red Sox had come alive. They were in a pennant race that they would eventually win. So, the Major's daughter got tickets to Fenway Park. The Red Sox were playing the Yankees. Yaz, as he was known throughout New England, was in left field, Rico Petrocelli, another favorite of mine was at shortstop, and their best pitcher, Jim Longborg, was on the mound. Rico hit a two-run homer, and the Red Sox beat the hated Yankees 3-1. Fenway Park was packed, and the place was bedlam at the end of the game. I had a great time and then retired to the Fenway Motor Inn.

On my last night, I went out with my sister, Joan. She had flown up from Texas to wish me well. Although she was a half-sister from my father's first marriage, we were close. She had always been supportive and had helped me in my early years. In fact, she had found me when I fell down a steep ravine and applied first aid. Later, she taught me to swim and introduced me to the game of baseball. We really cared for one another. I appreciated that she had flown up to see me off and wanted this evening to be light and fun. I had picked out a nightclub not too far from our hometown. They had a Dixieland band, and the music was very uplifting, led by an exceptionally good banjo player. We arrived at the club and enjoyed a few drinks as the band was playing many good tunes from the past. We were having a good time. But like storm clouds rolling in on a bright summer day, the reason for our get together was approaching. I led off with what needed to be done in the event I did not return.

    I told Joan that I wanted things to be as smooth as possible for my mother. Joan nodded to this obvious request. I told her that my desk held my bank account and my will. She listened intently with a sadness crossing over her face. Then I launched into my desire as to how my funeral should be conducted. I wanted to be buried in my dress blue uniform in the church my family members had attended since the 1600s. The burial would be in the family cemetery, and it would be a military funeral. At this point, tears started to roll down her cheeks, and I was touched. So, as the band launched into a snappy rendition of "The Darktown Strutters Ball," and everyone was singing along, we sat there with tears flowing. It was indicative of the times, and the swirling emotions surrounding the coming events.

**My Sister
Joan Griswold Park**

The Flight to Combat

The next day I said goodbye to my mother. We had both been prepared for this moment and thus kept control of our emotions. I hugged and told her not to worry. She smiled and said, I love you. I walked out quickly to avoid any more emotion and was driven to New York by a friend. I boarded a United Airlines flight. It was a commercial flight headed to Hawaii with a brief stopover in LA. Almost all the people were going to Hawaii, and they were in a festive mood. Everyone was dressed in loud shirts and colorful blouses. As the plane leveled off and reached cruising speed over New York, the people began to engage in banter about their destination. What islands are you visiting? Where are you staying? What restaurants do you recommend? Have you been there before? Everyone was excited and happy.

Since my destination was decidedly different, I said nothing. All I could think about was my poor mother. I loved her dearly. She had been so good to me after my Dad died. Always supportive. Not many mothers would have visited 15 schools to upgrade my education. I was her only child, and with my Dad gone, I was the focus in her life. I never wanted to hurt her. But I had. In my great desire to make something of myself and embark on this great adventure, I would bring her so much stress. Although she had hidden it from me, it was obvious that her only child going off to combat in the Marines would be awfully hard on her. I was troubled by the thought that she was sad—this, combined with the realization that I might not be returning, dampened my mood considerably.

Meanwhile, my seatmate was a pleasant middle-aged woman. She was going to Hawaii and was chatting with her friend to her right. I think she felt the need to say something to me.

"Are you in the service?" she asked—a rather keen observation since I was in my Marine Corps uniform.

"Yes," I said.

"Off to Hawaii?" she responded.

"No," I said with a touch of envy.

"Then you must be going to L.A, do you have friends there?"

"No," I replied. "LA is just a stopover. I am going to Vietnam."

"Vietnam," the women appeared puzzled. "Isn't that where the war is?"

"Yes," I replied. There was an awkward pause.

"Well, good luck."

I thought this reply odd. Good luck as if I was going off to summer camp. The whole conversation was strange. The women were genuinely nice; there were no anti-war feelings. Those would come later—just a total disconnect. Here I was having been told by my sergeant instructors that everything I did would have consequences in a life and death situation. Also, we had been told to get our personal effects together since some of us would not be returning. We were fighting for the survival of freedom and the American way. That was the general feeling in the military. Yet, for the public, the war was far off. Something that they had heard about, but it did not directly affect them and certainly did not affect their way of life. No one was asking for any service. It was not like World War II when everyone made great sacrifices for the cause. President Johnson had promised both guns and butter. A successful war with little or no sacrifice or commitment on the part of the American people. I suppose it was a good political position. Still, it was hard for a young military person to digest and understand. The whole conversation just served to illustrate how different this war was being perceived than previous ones. In a short time, this disconnect would explode across the country.

We arrived for the stopover in LA, and I got off the plane. I wished the lady next to me a pleasant time in Hawaii, and she again wished me good luck. I just smiled.

In LA, I met up with other Marines who had flown in from all over the country. Bear was there from Ohio. Other members of our training platoon were there as well. The next day we boarded buses and headed to Travis Air Force base just south of San Francisco. I had never been to California before and marveled at how different it was from New England. I had always taken large trees for granted, but in LA, what we would consider a small tree was a big deal. Then there were hills with rocks, scrub brush, and small palm trees. It was pretty in a quite different way. I still preferred New England. Then there was the traffic. A four lane road was a big highway back east, but here eight lanes were common. Cars flew everywhere with intersecting freeways. It was hard to imagine where everyone was going. Freeways to nowhere were my observation.

Our buses arrived at Travis, and we boarded a large Air Force jet that was headed to Okinawa. Seating was by rank. The officers sat upfront with the Non-commission officer (sergeants) next, and the troops filled up the rest of the plane. The plane taxied down the runway and headed out into the Pacific. I looked out the window and saw the land disappearing. It struck me at that moment that I was leaving the United States and might not return. It produced mixed feelings. I had no reservations regarding my commitment to the Marine Corps. I had been well trained and looked forward to the opportunity to lead Marines.

On the other hand, of course, I did not want to die. I just rationalized that it wouldn't happen. Again, mixed feelings.

The officers were quiet. The non-commissioned officers talked in soft tones. They were more seasoned, with many having already seen combat. They had a good idea of what was happening. As for the troops, there was nervous chatter. Many tried to cover their fears with talks of their last night in the US. All had lots to drink, and many had tales of sexual adventures. They laughed and kidded each other, but it was nervous laughter. For some, this was a return to the Nam, and this time it would be worse. This was no longer an advisory role. Two reinforced Marine Divisions were involved in a war that was heating up by the day. As for me, I tried not to think too much, but sleep was not possible.

Okinawa

The flight seemed endless—thirteen hours in the sky following the sun. I was exhausted. We flew into Wake Island for a brief refueling. I was amazed at how small the Island was. It seemed the runway took up half the island. It was hard for me to believe there had been a major battle fought there in World War II. Refueled, we left Wake and arrived at Kadena, Air Force Base in Okinawa. Okinawa was vastly different from the States. Kadena was a nice base. The Air Force always had nice bases. Whoever lobbied for their budgets, sure knew what they were doing. Put on buses, we headed to the northern part of the island. We passed a big Navy base and a modest Army base. As we traveled farther north, the island turned poorer. Typically, the Marines were in the worst section with the worse facilities. As opposed to the Air Force, who always went first class, the Marines prided themselves with doing more with less, and we always had Spartan conditions. With that understanding, we pulled into Camp Hanson at the Northernmost part of Okinawa. It was so desolate; I would not be surprised if Japanese soldiers were in the area thinking World War II was still on.

Camp Hanson was a staging area for Vietnam. Here our uniforms would be stored along with our civilian clothes. Four sets of combat utilities were issued, along with two sets of jungle boots and various equipment. We attended lectures on recent operations and were shown very confidential maps that indicated the latest positions of major units in-country. Our units were marked in blue, the enemies in red. Vietnam was divided into four sectors by roman numerals I-IV- North to South. Since the Marines were in the first sector, it came to be known as I corps. In I corps, the 3rd Marine Division was headquartered in the city of Quang Tri just below the DMZ and west to a little spot called Khe Sahn and south to Hue City. Khe Sahn would become one of the biggest battles of the war. The First Marine Division was headquartered in the coastal city of Danang and extend north past Phu Bai, west towards the Laotian border, and south to An Hoa and Chu Lai. Those towns and cities, which meant absolutely nothing at the time, would come to be burned in my memory forever.

The interesting part of Camp Hanson was not the camp itself, which was pretty standard as an old typical military base, but the town right next to the camp. Kin Village. Kin Village was a collection of bars, whorehouses, bars, and more whorehouses. Walking into Kin Village, I had never experienced anything like it. First, the colors of the two-story cinderblock buildings were hard on the eyes. These were not the soft pinks of Bermuda or the tearful grays of Nantucket. They were bright reds, greens, yellows, purples, lavenders. My mother's favorite word, tacky came to mind. I had to smile.

Second, were the names of the bars. All were stateside names like Detroit City, Killers, Lady Luck, and of course, Hot Girls, Easy Times, Lovers, etc. I had seen Tijuana, Mexico, and Kin Village made Tijuana look classy. But by far, the biggest adjustment was the open sewer ditches. They flowed alongside the streets, and the smells were staggering. The streets were dirty, no filthy would be more to the point. The bars were dark, dingy, and loud. They served watered-down drinks, warm beer, and warmer Japanese wine. Then there were the girls. They were everywhere, all yelling in broken English what they would do for you or to you. If it sounds enticing, it wasn't. They were not particularly attractive, they were unkempt, and it was not hard to imagine them with all kinds of diseases. I was turned off by the whole sight. I returned to Camp Hansen with a really bad opinion of Kin Village.

Six months in Vietnam would greatly alter that opinion.

Welcome to the Nam

Assignments

The time had come. Bear and I, along with maybe 30 others, found ourselves in the Officer's Club at Camp Hansen around 2200 hours (10 o' clock-PM). We each took a shot of whiskey, said a brief prayer, shook hands with the words Semper Fi (short for Semper Fidelis, Latin for Always Faithful, which is the Marine Corps motto), and headed out the door. Soon we were in a small plane headed to the airbase at Danang, Vietnam. It was quiet, everyone lost in their thoughts. I had never been a heavy thinker who did a great deal of long-range planning. I tended to live for the moment, enjoying what life brought. Up to now, life had brought me a great deal of joy. My prep school and college roommates, sports, training with great guys, funny events, welcome home parties, Donna, and the Major's daughter, were all simply good fun. But somewhere in the far reaches of my brain where I did not like to go, it was coming to the realization that the party was about to end. Casualty figures were escalating, and the Marines in I Corps were locked in heavy combat with an enemy that no one understood, and everyone had greatly underestimated, especially in Washington. The prevailing thought that American firepower would cause the enemy to flee back to North Vietnam and settle for a quick peace was not going to plan. As time progressed, it never did.

The pilot announced

"We are 20 miles off the Vietnam coast. We will be coming in fast, get off quickly, we do not like sitting on the runway."

We peered out the windows. In the distance, I saw flashes of lights in the sky. Flares, artillery, and rockets, it looked like the Fourth of July.

"Dead by Halloween," was Bear's comment to me.

Gallows humor was one way to deal with the tension, and in time everyone in combat engages in it. The pilot drove the small plane on the runway, we scrambled off. I was hit with a blast of hot air from the airfield. The plane took off, back to Okinawa. We were hurried into a building where we were checked off and sent to a group of tents near the runway. It was around midnight, and it was hot. This was September in the Nam. It was also dusty, and it was incredibly loud. All night long Marine Corps F-4 phantom jets roared into the night. Bear and I were on cots with little time to sleep. It was my first night in the Nam. Like many to come, the weather was uncomfortable, confusion was all around, and there was an air of uncertainty that hung in the air. Only 13 months to go!

The next day, it rained. That immediately turned the dust into mud, but the heat was on the rise. Humidity was thick. It reminded me of Louisiana in the summer. We went to another building to get our orders. I hoped Bear and I would be together. We had been together since the start and were close. Not to be.

"Third Division," said the Marine administrator to Bear followed by "First Division" to me.

We would be at opposite ends of the I Corps. Bear would board a chopper to head north, and a jeep pulled up to deliver me to my unit. Bear reached into his pocket and took out a dollar. This was done a lot in the Nam among friends. He tore the dollar down the middle, splitting our first President in two. He stuffed part in his pocket and gave me the other.

"When we get back to the states, we will tape it together and have a drink," he said.

I agreed, and he disappeared. I hoped it would not be the last time we would be together.

Staff Sergeant Ron

My driver, a Marine lance corporal, picked me up, and we headed west out of the airport, away from the sea. We passed grass huts which served as homes for the Vietnamese. Then out into the country. We saw an ARVN Camp. ARVN being the South Vietnamese Army. The camp did not appear too military.

"Watch out for those guys," counseled my driver.

That would be the first of many warnings that our South Vietnamese allies were less than what I had been led to believe.

The driver continued west as we headed for the base of a large mountain range. Slowing down, he identified First Tanks on our left, Seventh Engineers on our right. We were between these Battalions. He pulled into our base camp, 11th Motor Transport Battalion. I reported to the Operations Officer, a captain who told me I would be assigned to Charlie-"C" company and command the second platoon.

"Your company commander is Lt. Barry, and your platoon sergeant is SSgt Ron."

When he mentioned SSgt Ron, a look of disdain crossed his face, "Good luck."

After leaving his office, I was instructed to go to supply and get my gear. At supply, I was given a helmet, flak jacket, cartridge belt, and then told to report to the weapons bunker. At weapons, I got a 45-caliber pistol and a 12-gauge shotgun. Also, I asked for a grenade launcher. Sergeant Tom back at Lejeune had told me there was nothing better than a grenade launcher for breaking up an ambush. The weapons sergeant said it was unusual, but he complied.

I went down to the office of C company to report in. The first sergeant met me and welcomed me aboard. A veteran of Korea, he had weathered features and had a hard look. But he liked officers if they kept him out of the field.

"Lt Barry is out on a convoy. I will introduce you to your platoon sergeant, SSgt Ron".

As he said, SSgt Ron, a strange smile crossed his face. "You will find him-unusual."

Who was this SSgt Ron?

SSgt Ron stood at attention as I was introduced. He did not salute as that was forbidden in Nam. Snipers loved to take shots at officers. Lt. Dan, the officer who told his men to never salute officers in the field in *Forest Gump,* got that right. But SSgt Ron did stick out his exceptionally large hand,

"Welcome to the Nam, Lieutenant."

SSgt Ron was around 5' 10" and 200. He was stocky with a barrel chest, and huge forearms, Popeye type arms. He was a little heavy but very muscular. His eyes were bright and sharp. He looked at me with a slight smile as if to say I am a professional Marine, and I know what I am doing. He exuded strength with a hint of cockiness.

After sizing me up as a new Lieutenant, he continued:

"You will not have any problems with Second Platoon," he said with a great deal of confidence.

There was a reason for that. As I was to learn, SSgt Ron had two great passions in life. The first was fighting. SSgt Ron loved to fight, and he was good at it. Along with his large beefy arms and 200 muscular pounds, he was very quick for a large man. Combine his physical strengths with a hair-trigger temper, and you have an extremely dangerous individual. While most men needed a provocation to fight,

SSgt Ron reversed that premise. SSgt Ron sought out reasons to fight. A failure to comply with any request, a dirty weapon, or even the wrong look was all it took. As I was to learn, the men in the platoon viewed him with mixed emotions.

On the one hand, they respected his strength, toughness, and combat record. Marines often would argue about who had the toughest sergeants, and most would agree SSgt Ron would win any debate. If you did your job, he was fair, and being hard was OK. If you cut corners or lacked aggression in combat, SSgt Ron could be terrifying. One thing for sure, no one would ever challenge what was demanded by SSgt Ron.

SSgt Ron's second great love was women. His standards were not too high. Any women qualified. He had not been back to the states in five years. He rotated back and forth from Vietnam to Okinawa. Between these two spots, his exploits were legendary. He was known to have three women in a day, and sometimes to use the gambling parlance, he would double down having two at once. As a result of these conquests, SSgt Ron was not well-liked by officers. The fighting caused paperwork and complaints, especially when he physically attacked Navy and Air Force personnel. The whoring was a bad example for the men. Venereal disease was a big problem, and Sergeants were supposed to set an example. SSgt Ron was a problem for officers, and the feeling had become mutual. SSgt Ron distrusted most officers from a fighting standpoint and felt most of them were pussies. A term he used with many connotations. What SSgt Ron really prayed for was an officer who would appreciate his fighting spirit and look the other way at his love of the ladies. His prayers were about to be answered.

I immediately liked SSgt Ron. First, Marines were supposed to fight. And while beating people in night clubs was maybe not ideal, getting troops in line was essential. One must understand the Marines of this period. Many came from very troubled and hard backgrounds. This was still the days of the judge saying:

"Well son, you have a choice. Jail or the Marine Corps."

Almost all opted for the Marines. They may have been well disciplined in boot camp, but out in the Nam with killing all around them, they could become difficult if not effectively managed. Trying to explain a difficult combat environment to a 17-year-old tough kid could be a challenge. But with SSgt Ron next to me, I could say anything. There would be no questions, or SSgt Ron would have a "discussion" behind the tents. It only took a few of those meetings, and my message was received.

Then there was combat. While SSgt Ron could beat up on service members, it was really a warmup for what he could deliver to the enemy. One time in a firefight, an M-60 machine gun jammed, and the machine gunner struggled to clear the weapon. As the story goes, the enemy was advancing. Without hesitation, SSgt Ron leaped up, exposing himself to enemy fire, pushed the gunner aside, and in seconds cleared the round, chambered the band of bullets, and began firing. He must have single handedly killed five NVA that day. The officer in change wanted to put him up for a medal, but SSgt Ron lobbied for a three-day pass to Okinawa to service two sisters. This was my kind of Marine.

And that led back to his second love. While most officers found his whoring a bad example, I was mesmerized by his conquests. As a small boy is drawn to the accomplishments of athletic heroes, I found SSgt Ron's escapades to be of great interest. We would become a great team. With my leadership capabilities, SSgt Ron's ability to beat the living hell out of everyone, and our mutual love of the opposite sex, things were looking up in Second Platoon.

Lieutenant Barry

After becoming acquainted with my platoon sergeant, it was time to be introduced to the Commanding Officer of C Company, First Lieutenant Barry. Lt. Barry was from California, and he fit the image. Tall, blond, blue eyes, he had an easy-going nature about him. Lt. Barry loved to smoke crooks, which were black rum soaked cigars that were crooked; thus, the name crooks. Work needed to be done, and missions had to be accomplished, but he took a smooth approach. He would lean back with a crook and apply his motto of *Don't Make Waves*.

For many reasons, Lt. Barry was very popular, especially with the troops. Although a commanding officer does not spend much time with the troops, the fact that he didn't scream orders or hold multiple inspections went over well. The senior sergeants liked him because he delegated plenty of responsibilities to them and trusted them to get things done. That allowed the senior staff to get things done their way. Their way was to delegate to junior staff officers. The senior staff did not attend formations or meetings. Sleeping late and hitting the club early was the order of the day. Fellow officers from other platoons loved Lt. Barry. In a Marine Battalion, the four Company Commanders are always vying for the favor of the Battalion Command- "The Old Man." Marines are competitive, and the Commanders of Alpha Company and Bravo Company nearly came to blows to prove which one was better. Delta Company also sought favors. But there would be no threat from Charlie Company. Lt. Barry was content to fill assignments without picking favorites or seeking accolades. Behind his back, his fellow Commanders called him California Dreaming.

Meeting with his officers, California Dreaming spent as little time as possible on Marine matters. What he really enjoyed was informing us about the beaches in California. He must have known fifty of them and could expound on the pros and cons of each. Of all his many beaches, Lt. Barry said the best was Blacks Beach just north of San Diego and slightly south of Camp Pendleton. Camp Pendleton is the largest Marine Base on the California Coast. Blacks Beach, as our guide continued, was hard to find, and parking was difficult. Also, you had to scale down a cliff on a narrow path to get there. But the rewards were many. First, it had beautiful sand and long rolling waves for surfing. Not the surf that could hurl you on to the beach but those rolling waves that would gently glide you to the shore, much in line with his lifestyle. But the greatest part of Blacks Beach was it was a nude beach inhabited by many California girls who felt an all-around tan would propel them into key movie roles or at least a good shot at the casting director's couch. Many Marines patrolled Blacks Beach. It was a great combination. Marines in great shape with no adversity to taking off their clothes and women out for fun and whose principal goal was to acquire a tan. To the junior officers, Lt. Barry was a source of vital information.

Troops

A Marine platoon is approximately 40 men. We were slightly short-handed, so we were around 32. As a second lieutenant, I was the platoon commander—one of four lieutenants reporting to the company commander who was the first lieutenant. SSgt Ron was the platoon sergeant. There were three squad leaders: all enlisted men "E-5" Sergeants. They reported directly to SSgt Ron. They were all well trained and excellent Marines, but their personalities were quite different.

The first squad was Sergeant Roy. Sgt. Roy was from Florida and grew up farming in the orange groves. His family had been farmers for generations. Sgt Roy was in great shape. Around six feet, his body was thin and hard. He could march all day and never appear tired. Although he could not come close to SSgt Ron in terms of fighting, he was tough enough to keep anyone in his squad from challenging him. Sgt Roy was one of the most serious men I ever met. I do not think I ever saw him smile. He was deadly serious about everything and had little to say. Yes, Sir or No Sir was the extent of conversation I had with Sgt Roy. He was a little unnerving because you never knew what he was thinking. His eyes were cold and hard, with no brightness or sparkle. Yet, he really knew his job, especially as it pertained to weapons. The men in a squad tend to take on the personalities of their leader, and Sgt Roy's men were the best trained and most efficient in the platoon. They excelled in combat. Sgt Roy viewed combat as the reason he was in Vietnam. While he did not take unnecessary chances, he was always prepared and could deliver a devastating blow to the enemy. He did not appear to give killing much thought one way or another. It was simply a job that he was expected to perform. SSgt Ron liked him because he was organized, efficient, and in SSgt Ron's words "an effective killing machine."

The second Squad was Sergeant Ritt. Sgt Ritt was from the mid-west, around Indiana, I think. In many ways, he was the exact opposite of Sgt Roy. He was a large man but not as hard. He was jovial and liked to laugh. He had completed two years of college and dropped out only because his funds ran out. He planned to go back once his tour was up. Sgt Ritt was easy to talk to and enjoyed stimulating discussions. The purpose of the war was one topic he spoke of often. While he was 100% loyal, he had, on more than one occasion, questioned our role in Southeast Asia. In combat, Sgt Ritt was more inclined to err on the side of caution. He liked to call for mortars or artillery rather than charge headlong into a hostile situation. This attitude, coupled with thoughts on our overall missions and the fact that he was better educated than others, put a strained relationship between him and SSgt Ron. SSgt Ron called him the "Professor" and kept a close eye on him. From SSgt Ron's view, questioning the purpose of the war was not something that was done at our levels. In fact, at the platoon levels, it could be dangerous. There should never be any doubt whatsoever about an order. Discussions led to doubts, and doubts led to hesitation, and hesitation led to men dying.

"Don't think too much," was SSgt Ron's constant advice to the Professor.

For his part, Sgt Ritt was smart enough not to ever challenge SSgt Ron and would always obey his orders. Still, privately he confided his dislike of SSgt Ron's leadership style, which was based more on fear than respect. It was an interesting dynamic for me to observe. I liked both but for quite different reasons.

The third Squad was Sergeant Winstead. Sgt Winstead was a SSgt Ron in training. While he was not quite as dangerous, Sgt Winstead could hold his own, and like his role model, he loved to fight. He was loud, aggressive, and combative. SSgt Ron saw him as a protégé and encouraged his aggressive style, which did not need much encouragement. As Sgt Roy's men were trained and efficient, and Sgt Ritt's men were fun-loving and somewhat cautious in their style, Sgt Winstead's men bordered on the insane. They were more inclined to get into trouble, and fights were common. Whereas Sgt Roy regarded fights as disruptive to smooth operations, and Sgt Ritt thought they were stupid, Sgt Winstead's main concern was who won.

Along with fighting, one of the squad's favorite games was bayonet throwing. The game was to see who would flinch. A squad member would stick out a foot, and the other would throw his K-bar-a long, very sharp knife at his foot. The goal is how close he could come to your foot. If the other person filched or moved his foot, he lost. Sgt Winstead's men were extremely skilled at the game.

We all wore jungle boots. Jungle boots were designed to shed water. In fact, they had two small holes in the bottom of the boot to deal with the monsoon rains and water from the rice patties as well as the streams we had to cross. Also, they were light, and the sides were canvas. Believe it or not, the designers of the jungle boots had not factored knife throwing into the design. Therefore, they were not that hard, and sharp K-bars had little trouble penetrating the boot. It was not uncommon for Sgt Winstead's men to be at sick bay getting treated for knife wounds. Many platoon sergeants would have put a stop to this activity, but SSgt Ron felt it promoted a warrior spirit. His biggest concern was not with the wounds but with anyone who flinched. He felt they were pussies and often berated them if flinching reoccurred.

As I became more familiar with the platoon, I began to employ the squads based on the characteristics I have described. Upmost in my mind was my relationship with SSgt Ron. I did not want to go against him as his experience and skills in handling the troops was essential. On the other hand, I wanted to be fair and keep up morale. For obvious reason, SSgt Ron favored Sgt Winstead's squad, and he cut them more slack on daily assignments. Likewise, he had no problem with Sgt Roy's squad, which could be counted on to complete any assignment. However, he distrusted Sgt Ritt and would often put his troops on extended guard duty and worse latrine duty, which was not pleasant. I would, at times, intercede, and SSgt Ron would always go along as he followed the chain of command to the letter. But I know behind my back, he would play favorites, and that was not going to change. Although I wanted to be fair, I usually had to agree with him. While Sgt Ritt was great for a lively discussion, we were in combat, and complying with orders always came first. Besides, I had to worry about SSgt Ron and his thoughts and meet Lt. Barry's requirements. Plus, there were other platoon commanders in the company, and I did not want them to have the upper hand. Thus, in most cases, I would go along with SSgt Ron, and assignments were clear. The third squad was favored, followed by the first squad, and the second squad was last.

As for combat, I would deploy each squad based on the assignment. If we were going into an unknown area, it was best to lead with Sgt Roy. His squad was the most efficient and would respond appropriately. If we were assigned to a hostile area, you wanted Sgt Winstead's as they were the most aggressive. It was sweeps through the villages where you wanted Sgt Ritt. Village sweeps were incredibly challenging as it was impossible to tell the good guys from the bad guys. Here you wanted to err on the side of caution, and Sgt Ritt was best at being sure when force was needed. Killing innocent villagers, even under the pressures of combat, was to be avoided at all costs. The consequences would be a major public relations problem and most likely cost me my command, and perhaps a court-martial. Regardless of what may have been reported back in the states, we were careful not to harm civilians whenever possible.

In summation, all three squad sergeants were good leaders and very dependable, well-trained dedicated Marines. They just had different styles, and I remember my training from Sgt Tom back at Camp Lejeune. Get to know the men, respect their skills, and experience, and use them in the best way to accomplish the assigned missions.

Next in command were the fire team leaders. The fire team leaders were corporals. There were three fire teams per squad or nine fire team leaders in the platoon. Two stood out.

Corporal Jenson was in Sgt Ritt's squad and corporal Gillette in Sgt Winstead's. Corporal Jenson had been in college, and like Sgt, Ritt was smart and well-read. He liked books which was unusual. Most Marines were well versed in pornography, but not up to speed on the classics. *Does it have any sex in it* was the first question asked regarding any reading materials. Not only did Corporal Jenson read, but he smoked a pipe. He and Sgt Ritt were good friends and were often engaged in spirited conversation out of the view of SSgt Ron. The latter would have threatened bodily harm if he felt their discussions were interfering with any duties or assignments. Jenson was always asking questions such as:

"What college did you graduate from Lieutenant?" He was interested in my thoughts or opinions. I enjoyed talking with him but was careful not to get too close. Again, the shadow of SSgt Ron was never too far away, and my relationship with my platoon sergeant was far more important than a corporal in a fire team.

The other Corporal of note was Corporal Gillette. Corporal Gillette was the opposite of Corporal Jenson. Gillette had been a gang member in Los Angeles and was hard as nails. Of course, he was in Sgt Winstead's squad, where his aggressive spirit was encouraged. He probably would have been killed by now considering his penchant for street fights had he not joined the Marines. Corporate Gillette loved the Marine Corps and proudly wore Marine tattoos. His goal was to become a senior sergeant. In a firefight, you wanted Corporal Gillette. In the rear areas, Gillette was a piece of work. Urged on by both SSgt Ron and Sgt Winstead, Gillette was known to challenge troops in other units to fights. I tried to avoid witnessing his fights as that would put me in a difficult position of having to write up a combat Marine for what many considered a very minor infraction, but I was aware of them. Gillette had little use for anyone who was not a Marine and, on one occasion, had threatened to beat up a Navy medical corpsman. Since corpsmen were essential in combat, he was persuaded to redirect his aggression. Still, it took some pleas from those who might someday need the presence of a corpsman. On another occasion that I did happen to witness, Sgt Winstead was in a playful mood.

"Hey Gillette, you are supposed to be so tough, what would you do if I came at you with a knife?"

With that, Sgt Winstead took out his K-bar and thrust it at Gillette. Gillette just smiled. Sort of an evil grin.

"Try that again, Sergeant."

Sgt Winstead thrust the knife forward. What happened next was a blur. Gillette's right foot shot out, hitting the right hand of Sgt Winstead, the knife flying into the air. In an instant, Gillette was behind the Sergeant with his own K-bar out and pressed up against his throat.

"To answer your question," said the evil grinner, "I would slit your throat ear to ear."

"Nice work," said Sgt Winstead.

When he learned of the incident, SSgt Ron wanted Gillette to be promoted on the spot.

For me, witnessing this encounter, it was a startling revelation. At first glance, most of these men were average looking, sort of nondescript. If you saw them on the street, they might not warrant a second glance—just everyday young men. In high school, they could be on the athletic team but not the star player, just a supporting teammate. But make no mistake, the Marines had turned them into hard, trained killers. Growing up in an upperclass waspy family followed by prep school and college, I had never come across anyone who resembled these men. It was as if they came from another world. I wondered how much influence they would have on my life.

Now it was time to meet the rest of the platoon, the men I would lead into combat. They were the lance corporals and privates that filled out the remainder of the squads. They numbered between 25 to 30, depending on the rotations and casualty figures. Troops stood at attention while I inspected them and their rifles. They were young-17, 18, and 19. The average height was around 5'9" and maybe 160 pounds; they were wiry and strong. They represented all races and backgrounds, although there was a preponderance of Hispanics since the platoon had been formed in San Diego. The names Rodriquez, Martinez, and Gonzalez were prominent. Almost all came from low-income backgrounds. They really had little going for them in the states. Whether they were in the fields of California, the swamps, and mountains of the south or the ghettos of the inner cities, most had a very limited future. But the Marines changed that. They were now part of a prestigious, well-respected organization that offered a good future. Many would stay in and make careers of the Marines.

On their helmets were religious writings; Just you and me -right God, Jesus walks with me, and verses such as John 3:16. Along with the religious writings, many helmets had the Ace of Spades held by large rubber bands. The Vietnamese were suspicious, and the Ace of Spades is known as the card of death. The message was clear; attack us, and you will die.

Their faces were tanned by the sun, and many had tattoos on their arms. Three tattoos stood out: The Marine Corps eagle, globe, and anchor with the initials USMC underneath, also the Marine Corp bulldog with the Marine motto Semper Fi. The other tattoo which caught my attention was a sword with a sash around it. On the sash were the words "Death Before Dishonor." As I would come to learn, these men really meant this to a man. They would die not so much for a cause, or even for the country, but to uphold the values of the Marine Corps and to protect one another. I understood them and liked them. I would do everything possible to keep them alive.

Convoys

Convoys were one of my major responsibilities. All units had a few trucks to take care of their immediate needs. But we had over 50 five-ton trucks complete with wreckers and trailers. We were the principle resupply source for the entire First Marine Division. Ammunitions, food, medical supplies, spare parts, and the thousand little things that a military needs to perform in combat were moved by trucks. While helicopters could supply some materials, they were used mostly for transportation of troops. Troop deployment was a high priority, and Marines depended on us to supply the rest.

Our smaller supply operations comprised of 12 to 20 trucks in the 15 to 20-mile radius from Danang. The bigger ones were between 100 and 130 trucks that would go far into the north. These were major convoys, and all the vehicles and their support were controlled by senior lieutenants in our Battalion. New lieutenants were not ready for 120 truck convoys. I would start with a 12 truck convoy.

My first convoy was to Hill 10, directly west about 6 clicks (kilometers) from our position. It was held by the 1st Battalion, Seventh Marines, in the area known as Happy Valley. Marines were very sarcastic. Nothing happy ever happened in "Happy Valley."

We lined up all the trucks loaded with supplies and headed out the front gate. SSgt Ron was with me along with our radio operators and four Marine security teams. We were well equipped to resupply Hill 10. As we moved through the local villages, girls would wave, mostly at SSgt Ron. He smiled and waved back. I felt like I was with General Macarthur returning to the Philippines. The man was amazing.

Since Sgt Roy's squad had been on perimeter duty, his squad remained behind, and Sgt Ritt had split his squad because of other duties, so only a handful of his men were with us. That meant most of the men on this convoy were Sgt Winstead's. SSgt Ron was pleased as he preferred Winstead's crew. The men were primed and always ready for a fight.

"I hope we get attacked as I want to kill some gooks," was Gillette's comment to his team.

I was not quite so eager, but we were ready.

As we passed through the perimeter, the landscape changed, heading west into rolling hills. Everything seemed normal, but, in the Nam, you could never tell. Months earlier, on this very road, over 200 NVA had attacked a similar convoy, hitting them with rockets and mortars, destroying the trucks, taking the ammo, and killing most of the Marines. When I relayed this concern to SSgt Ron, he just laughed.

"Well, Lieutenant, when your times up, your times up. You worry too much," he added a Sir just to keep it proper.

I had to smile. Nothing phased this guy.

There were no problems. We delivered the supplies and came back. I practiced my radio commands to many units and felt it went well. My first venture into enemy territory was successfully in the books.

My second convoy was south in a different part of Vietnam. We passed an extremely poor area, the troops called Dogpatch. There were many huts in Dogpatch that housed the poor farmers of the area. Their huts were made of discarded materials from our military as well as straw gathered from the fields. The roofs were tin. The floors were dirt, and inside were the barest of essentials, a bed, and a few tables and chairs. It was shocking that so many would live in these conditions.

We moved past the villages into farm country. Along the way, I saw the locals for the first time. There were very few young males. Most young men were in the Army, our allies, I hoped. There were, however, many young children, and even more old men and women. It was hard to judge age as years in the sun had wrinkled their faces, but I would guess in their forties or early fifties; they did not live too much longer than that. Most chewed a beachy type of nut that blackened their teeth. The women would often be seen picking lice out of their hair and eating them. But by far, the worse visual was the lack of sanitation. With no restrooms or any facilities, the men and women just urinated and defecated by the roads, fields, and in the rice paddies. This visual, combined with the smells, had an immediate effect on the troops.

Simply put, they were repulsed and felt the Vietnamese were nothing short of animals. This may not have been fair, but keep in mind, you are dealing with 17 and 18-year-olds who had little training on the history and culture of the people. The government trained them to kill and gave them the weapons to do so, but they were ill-equipped to deal with the scenes they were witnessing. I came to realize that while Marines are great in combat, they were a poor choice to win the hearts and minds of the Vietnamese people. Anyway, the convoy went well, and we delivered our supplies and returned to base camp within the prescribed time frame.

My third convoy was far more challenging. We would be taking three large tanker trucks full of JP 6 aviation fuel along with the usual supplies over 20 miles south to An Hoa. This was dangerous territory, and it was raining hard to add to the challenge. Once south of Danang, we traveled to the Song Thu Bon River. We crossed it, into what was called the Arizona territory. More Marines died in the Arizona territory than any other area in Viet Nam. At this point, all kidding and conversation stopped. Men chambered rounds, and their eyes searched the area for trouble. Ahead was Hill 55, home to the 3rd Battalion, Fifth Marines. Two clicks to the south of us lay An Hoa right in the path of one of the direct routes of the Ho Chi Minh Trail. If the NVA and the Viet Cong could capture this area, they had a direct shot into Danang and the airbase that sent planes to the north. Standing in their way was the 5th Marine Regiment.

After being briefed at Hill 55, we moved slowly down a dirt road known as Liberty Road to the Marine base at An Hoa, home to the 1st Battalion, Fifth Marines. My friend Kel was there, and I looked forward to seeing him. It had been raining hard as we moved along a very muddy road. A truck swerved to avoid a pothole, and one of the tanker drivers hit the brakes too hard. The tanker jackknifed and slid into a ditch. We would have to get the wrecker to pull the big truck out of the ditch. This would be difficult under any circumstances, but the driving rain and the mud made it dangerous. As I directed the wrecker into place, we heard rifle fire. It was incoming-AK47's. Snipers were firing at us. Security returned fire while the drivers and mechanics worked frantically to get the tanker back on the road. It was dangerous, but what really concerned me was the possibility they had RPGs (rocket propelled grenades). If an RPG hit one of those tankers, we would be engulfed in flames. Forget body bags, there wouldn't be enough of us to fill a sandwich bag.

I called back to Hill 55, and they quickly sent a squad that moved out towards the firing. As was their style, the enemy broke and disappeared. Most likely, back to their safe sanctuary in Laos. We were spared, got the tanker back on the road, and delivered our supplies. This was my first time under enemy fire, and I felt I had done well. Scared, of course, but I called in the necessary support. It was only when I was safely back at camp that I realized the full consequence of standing next to a fuel truck with bullets flying.

By now, I was getting more experienced at running convoys. Lt. Barry felt I was ready for the larger ones that went North into Phi Bai and often on to Quan Tri, just south of the DMZ. These were large convoys between 80 and 120 trucks, and they were commanded by lieutenants platoon commanders.

The coordination of these events was complex and included many units with overall coordination at the First Marine Headquarters in Danang. As you passed farther north, overall control would be handed off to the Third Marine Division at Quan Tri. While captains, majors, and even colonels were aware of the convoys and monitored our progress, the movement of the trucks and troops fell on us. It was a lot of responsibility.

As these convoys left Danang, we would spend the night at camps and come back to Danang in a day or two. Trucks were loaded with equipment and supplies for troops, along with the everyday items that were needed for basic living requirements. Since Danang was the largest port in I corps, we were essentially supplying two Marine Divisions with materials.

I recall my first big convoy. We left our compound and went down to Route One, the main road and really the only large road that ran north to south. Lined up by the side of the road were 90 five-ton trucks and flatbeds. All were loaded with supplies from ammunitions, food, fuels, boots, clothes, and all kinds of parts to support all types of activities. The largest vehicles were the 18-wheel flatbeds loaded with pallets of supplies. It was a massive amount of material that had come into Danang by ship and were now loaded on to trucks ready to be taken to the camps at Phu Bai and other sites near the DMZ.

Ninety trucks meant 90 drivers, more like 120 since some vehicles had two Marines in them. There were three trucks of security personnel with approximately 40 more Marines. Then there were the supporting units. Between operations officers at our Battalion, Division leadership, air, artillery, and support units on call, along with Marine infantry units that we would pass through, there were at least 100 more Marines that were aware of what we were doing and where we were going. In total, 260 Marines would be involved in our convoy, and that did not include all the supporting units

People often ask me if I was scared in Nam. The answer is yes, but not as much with fear of the enemy. The real fear was I would make a mistake, and all these Marines would be in danger. That was my real fear. I had not slept much the night before the convoy. I went over, and over the call signs and the sectors we would travel through. I spent time with my sergeants and other lieutenants to be sure our orders were understood.

The strategy for controlling a 90 truck convoy was simple but efficient. We had a pace truck equipped with radios and a 50-caliber gun mount, with heavy armor. Their call sign was Charlie Pace. Then we had Charlie Trail at the end of the convoy, Then, near the end, was Charlie Maintenance with two large wreckers to pick up any brokendown trucks. Then we had Charlie Ex-ray. This was a jeep with a driver and two sergeants that would move up and down the convoy to spot any problems. Charlie's Ex-ray was invaluable for control. Finally, there was my jeep. I always felt I should be farther back in the convoy as it was easier to move up on a problem than go back. We had five contact points, all communicating on a single channel for control. It worked.

As I moved up to the trucks stationed along Route 1, radios crackled with radio checks conducted to ensure all communications were sound. There were checks to both Battalion and Division for control and assurances that support cover was available. That included artillery, air, and infantry units. When everyone was satisfied, and I had checked with all our Charlie units, I was convinced we were ready. I spoke to Charlie Pace.

"Charlie Pace, this is Charlie 6 over," I said.

"Charlie 6, this is Charlie Pace, over"

"Charlie Pace," move out.

"Roger, Charlie 6."

And with that, 90 five-ton trucks and flatbed trailers moved forward. The route was due north as we slowly moved out of the port of Danang and headed towards the ominous Hai Van Pass, which lay three miles up the road. The person who commanded this group was Lieutenant Griswold. It was scary but at the same time, exhilarating. To think that someone who was not considered prep-school material and had not followed in the family footsteps was now in a position to affect the lives of over 200 Marines and responsible for tons of supplies that would affect the lives of hundreds more.

I thought back to those who had believed in me: My parents, coaches, teachers, and friends. I was finally in a position of authority, and others were depending on me to bring them home safely. My self confidence was returning.

We continued to move forward from Danang and started to ascend into the Hai Van Pass. The Hai Van Pass has been described as one of the most dangerous roads in the world. Cut out from the side of the mountain, it is 5 miles long and rises 500 meters from sea level. The turns are hairpin, and the road is just wide enough for the large tractor-trailers to navigate. At some points, back wheels would be on the soft edge with a 400 to 500 meter drop off. There were no guard rails. The men who drove these vehicles were brave and skilled. It was dangerous in good weather. When it rained, it was even more dangerous. Sometimes near the top, we would be in the clouds, and that made visibility limited, which added to the danger. And that was just the road conditions.

As the road wound up into the mountain, jungle grass and vegetation came right to the edge of the road. It was thick and heavy. The enemy could hide in those thickets and would be impossible to detect. They could attack at any moment. If a mine or a rocket took out the pace truck, all vehicles would be halted. Then they could just throw hand grenades down on us. There had been attacks in the past, and we were on heightened alerts every time we went through the Pass.

With all this in mind, we continued to climb. One big concern was the breakdown of vehicles. Loaded with heavy supplies, the trucks belched black smoke as they labored up the steep inclines. If a truck overheated or had a mechanical failure, the maintenance team would immediately survey the situation. If necessary, the vehicle would be hooked up and taken to a checkpoint base. The vehicle and its supplies would then be picked up by another unit, perhaps the next day.

Under no circumstances were vehicles left on the road and certainly not in the Pass.

Upon reaching the top of the Pass, I would often pull over and watch the vehicles start the descent down the other side. In some ways, this was even more dangerous. Heavily loaded flatbed tractors would need to downshift and apply brakes to keep from going too fast and losing control. I recall looking back at a tractor bearing down on my jeep during the decent. If the air brakes failed and our jeep was hit, my driver and I would resemble the last scene in *Thelma and Louise*, where the two girls drove their car off a cliff. As in the movie, we would be shot over the cliff and into a rapid descent towards the South China Sea. Reaching the bottom of the Pass, I always breathed a sigh of relief and said a prayer of thanks that we had made it.

Stand-Off at the Bridge

After navigating the Hai Van Pass, our convoy headed north. We passed through some flat land that ran parallel to the water. I recall on one occasion; we were rolling along when suddenly I received a radio call from the pace vehicle.

"Charlie 6, Charlie 6, we have stopped on a bridge. Indigenous traffic is blocking us."

Soon the procession of 90 vehicles came to a halt. This was not good. I immediately told my jeep driver to speed up and pass the stopped trucks. We arrived at the scene. The bridge was narrow, and there was no room for our large 5-ton trucks to allow for the passage of the smaller Vietnamese buses, cars, and carts. An older Vietnamese gentleman was standing in the middle of the bridge facing the first truck (pace truck). Our driver was waving for him to move his vehicles off the bridge, but the old man did not move.

I came up to him and started to explain our situation. We must move all our vehicles across the bridge now.

"Supplies are needed up north," I said to the old man, "Many VC (Viet Cong) -you need to move now."

The old man argued in Vietnamese-I had no idea what he was saying, but he had many vehicles going south that must cross the bridge. I again tried to explain our position, but it was obvious that our conversation was going nowhere. Up to this point, SSgt Ron had been sitting in the jeep watching this discussion. Finally, he lost patience.

SSgt Ron reached under the seat and produced a 12-gauge shotgun. The gun was loaded. Without hesitation, he walked past me and pointed the gun at the old man's head. The old man stopped talking and stared at SSgt Ron. Slowly,

SSgt Ron lowered the gun and then approximately two feet in front of the old man, fired off two shots. Rocks, sand, and dust flew everywhere. The man turned and ran off the bridge, and all the vehicles turned around. In minutes, the bridge was clear. SSgt, Ron turned to me and smiled.

"Over here, Lieutenant, you need to get their attention first. Now you can move them out."

I gave a wave similar to what I had seen in a John Wayne movie to the drivers, and the convoy proceeded.

The rest of the trip went smoothly. We delivered our supplies to Phu Bai. That night as I lay by some sandbags next to a fox hole, I reflected on the bridge, and the strategy employed by my platoon sergeant.

What would have happened if the farmer had not moved or worse what would have happened if the weapon had misfired or SSgt Ron had jerked his hand and shot the farmer in the foot or the leg or, far worse, killed him? What then? And what role would I play in all of this? If I turned him in, I would be hated by the troops, and the higher command would blame me for losing control of the situation. I would be relieved of command and sent back to the States to serve out my time in a tiny cubicle, despised by all.

On the other hand, if I covered for SSgt Ron, it might slip by. But suppose the old farmer was an important leader or Village Chief? Then there would be an investigation. If found guilty, I would be sentenced to prison. I would be disgraced. I could never go home and face my family. I would have to change my name and move out west. Maybe take a job in a lumber mill. My life, as I know, it would be over. Either way, I would not come out ahead. We had not been trained or prepared for this type of scenario. We were told that the Vietnamese would welcome us and comply with all requests.

I was quickly learning that the Vietnamese felt a combination of confusion, distrust, and even anger towards us. I believed I needed more experienced advice, and thus I planned to speak with my Commanding Officer-Lt. Barry

Lt. Barry was doing paperwork as I knocked on his door back at our base camp.

"May I speak with you, Sir," I inquired.

"Sure, come on in," said a smiling Lt. Barry "What can I do for you, David? As I recall, we were discussing Los Angeles beaches, although you know I prefer the ones in San Diego."

With that, Lt. Barry pushed back and reached into his breast pocket, pulled out a run-soaked crooks cigar, and lit up.

"Well, Sir, I always enjoy the discussion of beaches, but this is about tactics."

Lt. Barry frowned. "Yes," he said with an air of annoyance.

"Sir, I had an incident last week on a convoy," and I proceeded to tell him about the bridge and the confrontation I had with the farmer and how SSgt Ron intervened.

"Well," said Lt. Barry, "It all worked out. You delivered the supplies and made it back without incident. Sounds like a successfully completed mission to me."

At that point, he blew a couple of smoke rings into the air.

"Yes," I said, "But what would have happened if..." and I ran through a few situations.

At this point, Lt. Barry was getting uncomfortable.

"You're asking me what would happen if SSgt Ron wounded or killed the farmer?" He asked.

"Yes, Sir," was my reply.

"Well, Lieutenant, that is why you are there; to see that doesn't happen. Any more questions?"

I could see that was the final answer, so I said:

"No, Sir," and thanked him for his time. I marched out of the office, and he went back to his paperwork.

In thinking through his answer, that was the standard answer of senior officers. Carry out your mission, protect your troops, and be sure nothing bad happens along the way. In trying to process this sequence of assignments, I felt I'd better have a discussion with my platoon sergeant to be sure "nothing bad happens."

It was a few days later, and SSgt Ron and I were in a jeep headed to the airfield to pick up some parts. It was a bright sunny day, and SSgt Ron was in a good mood as he drove along the dirt road. I thought this was the perfect time to tactfully bring up my concerns about the bridge confrontation.

"SSgt Ron, remember the farmer you confronted at the bridge on our last convoy," I asked.

"Yea," he said, "He sure ran when the shotgun went off," laughed SSgt Ron.

"Well, yes, he did, and it all worked out," I stated. "But what would have happened if he did not move?"

"What!" SSgt Ron was surprised at the thought. "Gooks always move when you point a weapon at them," he stated.

I am sure the thought of not moving never occurred to him. "I just suppose," I answered.

"Well," said SSgt Ron somewhat exasperated, "I would move him-I guess that would not have been a problem."

Obviously not. The farmer weighed maybe 85 pounds, and SSgt Ron was 200 pounds of solid muscle. He could have picked up the farmer with one hand. It was not much of a concern.

"Sure," I said, "You could physically move him, but suppose by accident you had misfired and shot him-then what?"

SSgt Ron's smile was gone, and there was no doubt I was heading into dangerous territory.

"Well, that didn't happen," was his tense reply.

I continued, "Yes, I know, but if he did not move and his people refused to get off the bridge-what then?"

"Then, Lieutenant," said an increasingly angry SSgt Ron, "I would consider him an enemy soldier, and I would have shot him and thrown him off the bridge. Does that answer your question, Sir?"

He was not happy. We rode in silence for a while. I am certain if I were an enlisted Marine, SSgt Ron would have screamed many profanities and probably hit me for bringing up the point. But being an officer, he held back and simply glared, but I noticed his left hand on the steering wheel was white as he squeezed the wheel in anger. Finally, SSgt Ron felt the need to break the tension.

"Look, Lieutenant, I realize you are fresh out of Quantico Officer's School, and they tell you how wonderful all the poor Vietnamese are-just hard-working farmers trying to survive. And maybe that was the case. But you don't know. He could have been a Viet Cong or a Viet Cong sympathizer. Hell, for all we know, he could have been a colonel in the North Vietnamese Army disguised as a farmer. These zips (another slang term referring to zippers for slanted eyes) are sneaky. While the two of you are having a polite discussion on the rules of the road, he has managed to stop a 90-truck convoy. His next move is to signal to a buddy, who relays a signal to the mountains and mortars and artillery rain down on us. In a matter of minutes, the convoy is in flames, needed supplies are lost, and worst of all, a bunch of good Marines are lying dead in the road. So yes, if he failed to get out of the way, I would have shot him, and he knew it, and that is why he moved."

"Well, that is a point to consider," I said.

"Damn right it is. Listen, Sir, this is my third tour in the Nam, and I know what I am doing. The book stuff is one thing, but out in the bush, it's kill or be killed; I prefer the former! You stick with me, and you will go home alive with a chest full of medals."

With that, he laughed, and I had to smile.

Thinking through the conversation, I had doubts if I had made an impression, but at least I had approached the subject. And it was complicated. The rules of war are fine when soldiers fight on battlefields distinguished by different uniforms. But when the enemy hides within the civilian population and dresses like them, it becomes far more complicated. And the rules of previous wars did not really come close to addressing the Nam. It concerned me that Washington was a little slow to grasp this reality.

Helicopter Fire

A few months later, another convoy nearly cost me my command. As always, it started out as routine. We were to take troops from 7th Marines south to kick off operation with units from 1st Marines. The objective was south of the large Marine Air Base at Danang. There were ten trucks in convoy. No one expected any trouble, but we were ready just in case. Three of the trucks stationed in convoy had large ring mounts with 50 caliber machine guns on them. The 50s were powerful weapons that could bring a large amount of firepower into a kill zone. The gunners would stand on the seat of the trucks and control the gun, which could swing around the ring mount. A key to this strategy was the gunner was offered a 360-degree radius to fire the weapon. As the trucks bounced around on dirt roads, it took a strong man, well-positioned on the seat, to accomplish this task. With that in mind, a sergeant had assigned the smallest man in the unit as the 50 gunner this day. That decision would come into question.

We left the confines of our base camp and passed through the villages of Danang. Soon we were out in the open areas consisting of villages and rice paddies. All seemed normal. As I was to learn, nothing was normal in the Nam. Without warning, a village opened fire on us. The troops in the trucks returned fire, and we kept going to get out of the ambush site. The three 50 gunners opened up as well to bring fire on the enemy. This was as they were trained, and the truck drivers faced with bullets being fired at them sped up. Soon the trucks were traveling at a high rate of speed to escape the incoming gunfire. That would have been fine except the small gunner on the 50 lost his footing and fell off the seat. Being short, his legs could not reach the floor of the truck, and thus he was hanging from the gun attached to the ring mount. As the truck sped forward, the gun swung wildly. Again, this might not have been a problem except his two thumbs were locked on the triggers of the 50-caliber gun. This was a problem. As the gun rotated around the ring mount, and the driver accelerated down the road, the 50 was shooting hundreds of rounds up into the air. This was noted by the helicopter pilots who were flying in to the area to deliver their ordnance to the attack. It was a miracle we did not shoot down one or more of our own helicopters.

All I could imagine is the court martial where it would be asked of the young Lieutenant, what were your men doing firing at our helicopters. It would be a quick end to my military career. By sheer luck, we failed to hit the helicopters, and the gunner finally dropped off the gun. We got out of the attack zone and delivered the troops to the operation. All were safe, and I am sure the helicopter pilot got a medal and probably a promotion for flying through "enemy" fire to accomplish his mission.

Convoys continued and were, for the most part, uneventful. I commanded many big ones going north, and we had to deal with snipers, mortars, and rocket attacks. In Phu Bai, one was worth remembering. After arriving at the Phu Bai base camp, I had been speaking with an officer in a tent about the enemy in the area. As we were talking, the sirens went off, and together we ran to a trench and dove in. Some rockets hit the base and exploded, but all in all, there was no major damage. However, when we returned to the tent where we were talking, it was gone, replaced by a smoldering crater. It had been a direct hit. Five minutes earlier, and we both would have been killed. I remember the words of SSgt Ron, when your times up, your times up; really no other way to handle it. I did say more than my usual prayers that night.

Patrols

Along with convoys and guarding the perimeter at night, we conducted daily patrols throughout our sector. While there was always a chance of enemy contact, it was rare. The main purpose was to be sure the enemy was not storing weapons or food that could be used as a staging point for a night attack. Since the trails were often mined, it was safer to walk through the rice paddies and up into the hills. It was slow and tiring as your boots would sink into the muck of the paddies. The hills were just as bad in a different way. Saw grass would cut your arms, and your sweat would sting the cuts. Leeches would attach to your body, and the men would take cigarette lighters to burn them off. Back in the bunkers or fox holes, rats and snakes were present, and getting bit would cause a serious health concern. Then there were diseases. We got shots for bacteria and took malaria tablets every two weeks.

In Nam, the weather, insects, animals, and diseases were almost as bad as the enemy. In some respects, they were even worse. The enemy offered a chance to retaliate and do what Marines were trained to do. But the weather and the insects could not be controlled and simply had to be endured. It just added to frustrations that grew as time passed.

On these small patrols, you would get to know the men well. There was a young African American from Detroit who wore blue sunglasses. Everyone called him Blue Lights. Another was an Indian from Arizona. He was great in the field and never seemed to mind the conditions, we called him Scout. Then a large Marine from Beaumont, Texas, who, of course, was called Tex. You really came to appreciate these men as you walked with them, never knowing what would happen next.

The patrols were endless and extremely tiring. Keep in mind, these were additional duties. Our main job was convoys, daily support of operational units, and guard duty at night. Patrols required additional time, and the conditions were terrible. No one wanted to go on patrols.

For my part, I was beginning to question what we were doing there in the first place. I was just a Second Lieutenant and not privileged to senior-level military strategies. But I feel my instincts were right and were later supported by those who reviewed the war.

To put it in football terminology, it was as if we were playing between the 40-yard lines; neither side was willing to go into the end zone. For the North Vietnamese and the Viet Cong to win the war from a military standpoint would require coming out of the mountains and down into our base camps. The amount of firepower we could bring on would be suicidal. They would have no chance, and they knew it. If we remained, there was no chance we would lose this war. But winning it would require a different strategy. We would have to chase the enemy into Laos and Cambodia and, most important, into North Vietnam. While that could be accomplished, again from a military standpoint, the political consequences were many, and none were good. I am sure it was noted at the highest levels that just a short 15 years earlier, UN and American troops in Korea under the leadership of General Macarthur went into North Korea with the intent of uniting all of Korea. The Chinese stated that crossing the 38th parallel would cause them to enter the war. Macarthur said that would never happen, and President Truman went along. That was a tragic miscalculation. On November 27th, 1950, over 300,000

Chinese troops entered the war. They forced the UN and American troops back into South Korea in a terrible defeat for our forces. The Marines had been trapped at the Chosen Reservoir and fought their way south, destroying six Chinese divisions in the process. Yet, it must be noted that losing ground is not a victory.

It was abundantly clear there was no burning desire to risk another Korea. And then there was Russia and what would they do? Therefore, the strategy was not to win the war as much as it was to hold the ground and wait for one of two things to happen. One, the South Vietnamese Army would take up the fight and hold off the North or second, the North Vietnamese would get tired of the fight and give up the struggle. In the end, neither of those scenarios would happen.

For the South Vietnamese to win the war would require a concerted effort by all. In the North, that was possible because they had no options. Ho Chi Minh was a ruthless dictator who had no qualms about killing citizens and tolerated no dissension. You served in the military, and you did exactly as you were told. Fear was a great motivator. To question was a death sentence. Further, the North was fighting to reunite the country. Regardless of the political implications, the desire to be one country was a strong force for the North.

But in the South, there was less commitment. Yes, they were fighting for democracy, but the democracy in Saigon was not exactly what our founders envisioned. There were corruption and constant turnover among leadership. The South Vietnam army was very splintered. Some units were well led and fought extremely well. Others were terrible and hardly fought at all. The U.S. threw more first-rate equipment at them, but the results were mixed.

For US commanders in the field, turning the fighting over to the South Vietnamese was dangerous. You did not know what to expect. Better to depend on the US troops. Therefore, with the US doing the lion's share of the fighting, the development of the South Vietnamese Army was not progressing anywhere near the expected rate that Washington had calculated. From my perspective, it appeared to be a truly long shot to think the South Vietnamese could hold off the North if we left.

As for the promises that the North Vietnamese would quit IE surrender, I am sure some of them under constant bombing and losing thousands in firefights might have been willing to quit; but that was not an option. Either you fought, or you would be executed. Fighting was a better choice. So, they kept pouring down the Ho Chi Minh Trail, and our winning the war seemed nowhere in sight.

At least that was my perspective and observation as I trudged through the rice paddies and the mountains. But I kept them to myself and did my best to carry out all assignments and keep my men alive. It would be many years later that I would come to grips with my theory of the 40-yard lines and how unfair it was to the military who were unduly criticized for not winning a war that was never designed to be won.

To Fire or Not to Fire

Patrols were ongoing in between our other assignments, but this particular one stood out. It combined the frustrations of patrolling with the issue at the bridge that was mentioned earlier.

There were nine of us, and our assignment was to move along a tree line adjacent to a rice paddy and make sure there was no unusual activity in the area. The unusual activity covered a wide variety of factors. Still, the two main things to look for were increases in food and supplies that could indicate a pending attack or changes in routines of the local population, which could indicate enemy in the area. As usual, we did not see anything out of the ordinary.

It was hot and humid as always, and we were weighed down with ammunition belts, canteens, first aid kits, K-bar knives, heavy flack jackets, and helmets. To add to our misery, we stayed just off the trails. We struggled to walk through the heavy vegetation that grew everywhere.

It was important to stay alert, but it was hard. Everyone was tired, and it was very doubtful we would encounter the enemy in the middle of the day. As a result, our minds tended to wander, and it produced a numbing effect. I just wanted it to be over and get back to base camp.

I was in the middle of nine Marines as we continued to move along our sector of responsibility. Suddenly and without warning, there was a loud explosion followed by a piercing yell.

"Oh my God, my leg," screamed a Marine.

It was a mine.

Immediately, two Marines rushed forward, and one jammed a needle with morphine into the injured man's leg. At the same time, another took his belt and made a tourniquet to slow the bleeding. A young private who had been in the country less than two months had the misfortune of stepping on a mine. The device exploded at ground level, and his shin was destroyed. It could have been worse. Many mines in our area were spring loaded. Called "Bouncing Bettys," they would spring up to around three feet in height before detonating. The goal was to explode in the area of your groin and destroy the most important part of a Marine's anatomy. Men that survived those mines would never again enjoy the pleasures of a woman.

When the mine exploded, our patrol came to an immediate halt and all faced outboard, preparing for a fight. But there would be no fight. No one was shooting at us. Any Marine will tell you they would much rather have a firefight where you could lash out at the enemy. A mine offered no retaliation, nothing to do but care for the wounded or the dead.

Then we saw a figure moving. It was a boy; I would guess around 15 years of age. He leaped up from the woods and started to run across our front- perhaps 300 feet from our position. Next to me, a seasoned corporal dropped to one knee and lined the running boy up in his sights. For a trained Marine, this was an easy shot. Marines qualify at 500 yards, and at 300 feet, it was a can't miss target.

The Corporal looked at me, and I locked in on him. We had a few seconds to decide. The question flashing through our minds: was this an enemy who had planted the mine or perhaps crossed the wires to set it off, or was it just a scared kid running away from an explosion, a very normal reaction?

Before I could say anything, the corporal lowered his weapon.

"I wasn't sure, sir," he said. I noticed a tear in his eye. He knew the injured private. They were friends, and now his friend would never have the use of his leg. He would be medevacked out of Nam and survive, but the mine would take its' toll.

For the corporal, his tear represented the total frustration of the times. He wanted to fight; he was trained to fight. His friend had been hurt, and he wanted to avenge the loss. But on the other hand, he did not want to shoot an innocent boy.

As it turned out, the corporal made the right call. I was relieved, and the incident was over. But I was faced with the dilemma of what I would have done if he had shot the boy. And this was the frustration that we endured, just as the troops in the Middle East endure the same things today. It is very easy to make judgments and find fault when you are sitting in a secure area back in the states, but when you are in combat and adrenalin is pumping through your body and your friends have been hurt or killed, it is not so easy.

For me, trying to process what is the right response can really get inside your head. It is why I am extremely reluctant to speak about the war from a combat sense. I will tell funny stories or share the respect I had for the men I served with, but to try and go deep into the moral dilemmas that war can produce is very difficult. I believe most combat veterans will say the same thing.

China Beach

If the Viet Nam war was confusing to people in the states, China Beach is a perfect illustration of how strange and confusing the war was to us.

China Beach was a beach slightly north of Danang, where our unit was headquartered. At China Beach, there was a large USO building, and units would rotate on what was described as an "in-country R&R -Rest and Recuperation." Approximately every three months, a unit would spend a few days at China Beach.

It was our turn, and most troops, along with a few officers piled into trucks and headed to China Beach. The beach had beautiful sand like the west coast of Florida, and there were large trees near the water that provided for shade. There were picnic tables and a net for volleyball. There was a horseshoe pit, footballs, and wiffle balls. There was plenty of cold beer and sodas. In another section, cooks had steaks on the grills. There were loads of potato salads and fresh vegetables. Perhaps best of all were the large amounts of ice cream. The whole scene was something one would see at a family reunion at the beach. Considering we had been eating C rations, which were canned foods, and had not had any steaks, fresh fruit, or vegetables, it was a welcoming feast.

For the troops, this was paradise. Along with the food and beer, swimming was the major activity, as the saltwater helped to heal up sores and scars from the jungle. Other troops played volleyball and horseshoes. It was striking that away from the war and all the weapons, these were just teenage boys enjoying a day at the beach. There was such an innocence to the scene that one forgot that these young men were capable and trained to attack and annihilate an enemy.

For the officers, there were mixed feelings. On the one hand, it was very enjoyable. We, too, enjoyed the beautiful day, the food, and the relaxation away from the everyday grind and pressure of the war. However, there was always the concern that some troops would over indulge, and that was bad for many reasons. I worked closely with SSgt Ron to be sure that our platoon had fun but did not get out of line.

Further, for us, the war was never far away. At any time, a call could come in that we were needed. If that happened, we would have to round everyone up and head back to the base camp. Fortunately, that did not happen.

But the really strange part of China Beach was the total contrast to our usual routine. One minute we were on patrol or a convoy with the possibility of enemy contact, and within hours, we were at a beach that resembled Spring Break. It was most amazing to stand on the beach with the bright sun shining on us and in the distance, watching aircraft drop bombs on an advancing enemy. It was surreal. I felt like we were in an outdoor theater watching a movie off in the distance. Again, I thought of the forty-yard lines. We were in one area, and they were in another, and we fought in the middle.

A Strong Arm

This event was so terrifying to me that I had buried it deep in my mind and had not thought about it in years until I was completing the writing of my accounts of the war. However, I am sure it is the reason I am uneasy flying today, particularly on takeoffs. As an example of my fear of flying, I was on a commercial flight around five years ago flying out of Newark Airport. As the plane took off, we were buffeted by crosswinds, and the plane bounced around, something I always dislike. But then the pilot banked the plane hard to the left to follow the flight plan. I found my hands shaking, and I was sweating profusely. It had to be my mind's reaction to the Nam over fifty years ago.

The event began on a day at the combat base at Phu Bai. As a result of troop relocations back to the states, we were sometimes understaffed to provide support to troops in the field. Often, we would be required to double up on assignments as more and more supplies and equipment were needed to expand operations.

On this day, I led a convoy of trucks from Danang into Phu Bai for resupplies. Normally, I would have waited for the trucks to be unloaded and gone back with the convoy. But I was needed back at base camp for another assignment, so I caught a ride on a helicopter out of Phu Bai; headed back to Danang.

This was considered a routine trip if there was such a thing. I climbed aboard the chopper and sat down on the metal deck. The deck was wet with water and blood that had been spilled from three wounded Marines headed back to Danang for more medical treatment. A very large sergeant was with them. To my right was a machine gunner standing next to an

M-60 machine gun that was mounted on a tripod. Both side doors were open to allow for firing capabilities and to help offset the intense heat. Upfront was the pilot and a co-pilot.

We took off in the usual dust of Phu Bai and flew south towards Danang. The flight was moving quickly over treetops and rice paddies. Flying in helicopters was not fun. They could jerk from one side to another, and the roar of the engines and the rotation of blades made it almost impossible to hear. Far worse, they were easy targets. Small arms fire could cause serious problems if they hit the rotors, and an RPG could explode an entire chopper in a massive ball of flames. I had the horrible experience of watching one get hit. The chopper spun out of control and crashed to the ground. It burst into flames, and all the Marines aboard were killed. I tried not to think of that scene as we continued our flight.

Suddenly, I felt a thud, and almost instantly, our machine gunner began firing. We were under enemy fire. The noise of the machine gun was deafening, and the spent carriages bounced off my helmet and flak jacket. A few hit my arm and stung from the force and the heat. I was powerless to respond as we were just one big target moving across the skyline. There was no communication; just looks of fear exchanged by all of us.

The pilot banked the chopper hard to the left and headed out towards the sea to avoid the incoming fire. At that moment, I started to slide on the wet deck. I was headed for the open door. Instead of a sky, I could see the land rushing towards us. I was desperately looking for something to grab to stop my slide. It happened so fast; it was a blur of thoughts. Suddenly, seemly out of nowhere, a large arm reached out and grabbed me. I stopped sliding, the pilot leveled off, and we were out of danger.

I was so traumatized by this event that I was numb. I just sat on that deck shaking. I did not say a word. The pilot landed at the hospital facility in Danang, and medical personnel quickly took charge of the three injured Marines on my right, and I exited to my left. I turned around to thank the sergeant who had saved me from falling out, but he was gone. I never saw him again. I owed him my life, and he was gone.

Years later, in the seventies, when racial tensions boiled over in America, I would remember that incident because the arm that reached out to save me was black.

Embarkation School

Time passed, and I had been out in the field for six months. Lt. Barry liked me perhaps because I was such a student of California beaches. Anyway, he said I needed a break and put me in for Embarkation School in Okinawa. Sounded good to me.

Arriving in Okinawa, I learned that embarkation is what officers do to load a ship. The Marines worked closely with the Navy to accomplish this goal. A key was to be sure the weight that went into the ship was evenly balanced. Too much to one side would cause the ship to list, and that could be dangerous in a storm.

Today all the calculations would be done by computers, but back then, it was done with calculators. Sitting in class, we would look up the weight of a certain piece of equipment and then balance the weights of tanks, artillery pieces, trucks, fuel, and pallets of suppliers to each side of the ship. There were many contingencies. Fuel could not be stored next to ammo. Large vehicles had to be chained down, and those chains had to be calculated in terms of space. Considering I flunked math in high school and avoided it altogether in college, I was perhaps the worst officer in the Marine Corps to be in embarkation school. I was certainly the worst in the class. The Major who ran the class told me if I ever loaded a ship, there would be no doubt the ship would leave port, sail 300 feet into the bay, tip over, and sink!

As a result of the major's assessment, my days at embarkation school had been reduced to cutting out cardboard templates of vehicles, a skill I had mastered in the third grade. Not overly challenged, I turned my attention to Kin Village. Perhaps I had been too hasty in my first assessment.

In re-entering Kin Village, it took me less than five minutes to realize Kin Village had not changed; but I had. On my first visit, I had compared the village to the states. But now I had a new reference point-the Nam. So, I swung into the first bar to contemplate the situation. While the women did not compare to the states, no one had black teeth, no lice, and although there were open sewers, they did have toilets and knew how to use them. Then there was the fact that there were no mines in the streets, no one sniping at you, no rockets, and no one was going to slip into your compound and knife you. As I contemplated this, Kin Village looked better and better. In fact, as I finished my third beer, Kin Village was beginning to look a lot like Main Street, Disneyland. I could see Mickey and Minnie Mouse hand in hand, skipping down the Main Street of Kin Village waving to all the pimps and prostitutes. I wonder what old Walt would have thought of that.

So, fueled by the good folks at Budweiser, I reentered Kin Village. There is no need to go into any detail.

The Tet Offensive

With a few days to go at embarkation school, word reached us of the Tet Offensive. During the Vietnamese New Year celebration, the North Vietnamese infiltrated the south and staged uprisings throughout the country. U.S. forces and our allies were caught by surprise. As a result, all hands were needed, and we were put on a plane and thrown back into the war.

Upon arriving at Danang, it was a different scene. Marines were everywhere, and I was quickly taken to my unit. As the Marines gathered themselves and started the retaking of the villages and territories, the biggest fight was in Hue City. Known as the "Perfumed City," Hue was an ancient capital and a beautiful place. I had been through it many times and marveled at how clean and pretty it was especially compared to the rest of the country.

Perhaps because of its beauty and lack of strategic significance from a military perspective, Hue had avoided the war. The people of Hue went about their business, and the little shops and cafes were more reminiscent of the French influence than the Vietnamese farmers laboring in the rice paddies.

There were some troops in Hue made up of on an ARVN unit, a group of Marines guarding a compound, and a platoon of MPs. From my perspective, the MP's were more involved in traffic control than in any fighting. The enemy just wasn't there. But during the Tet Offensive, that changed.

The enemy brought in thousands of troops disguised as local peasants. One might think that the ARVN unit and perhaps the MPs might have been aware of 10,000 young men entering the city, but apparently, they had no idea. Hard to imagine.

But that is exactly what happened on the night of the Tet New Year. This event came to be known to all of us now as the start of the Tet Offensive. Approximately 10,000 North Vietnam's regulars simply took over the city. The beautiful old city of Hue was now a North Vietnamese stronghold.

As Tet caught everyone off guard, the situation at Hue must rank as the largest and least anticipated surprise. No warning or intelligence predicted the size of the enemy force. When the fighting started, the overwhelmed MP unit, and the Marines at the compound, radioed back to the Phu Bai base camp that there were some problems at Hue. The base commander figured some snipers were involved and sent a company of Marines from First Battalion; First Marine's up Route One to Hue to take care of their minor problem. What the men of 1/1 stumbled into was incredible. One company made up of approximately 200 Marines found themselves up against a dug-in enemy regiment of 10,000 North Vietnamese Regulars (NVA).

They immediately radioed back to Phu Bai that more Marines were needed. The Commanders at Phu Bai sent up another company. This time from First Battalion, Fifth Marines. Now around 450 Marines were battling 10,000 NVA. Needless to say, the Marines were pinned down and taking heavy causalities.

Slowly more and more troops were added, but with the NVA controlling over half the city, Marines had no choice but to turn their firepower on the enemy entrenched in Hue. First, Marines led the way, and we supported them. Day after day, we traveled north from Danang over the treacherous Hai Van Pass and into Phu Bai to resupply the Marines at Hue.

Sometimes we went from Phu Bai into Hue but not often as Route One was crowded with tanks, artillery, and hundreds of Vietnamese buses and cabs fleeing the city. It was pandemonium. As we made these runs, we were often sniped at, and mines were a problem. Many of our drivers received Purple Hearts for wounds. However, we accomplished our mission, and Hue was recaptured.

In the end, the North Vietnamese paid dearly for their attack. Our servicemen in-country had performed well. But back in the states, the fact that the enemy could mount such an attack after the military leaders had painted such a positive picture, did not sit well. Many considered the Tet Offensive to be the turning point of the war. However, we had no real sense of the home front, and for us, it was business as usual.

In retrospect, the most telling sight for me surrounding the Battle of Hue were the trucks loaded with Marines that we saw going in and out of Hue. The difference in the troops was startling. I thought it would have been a great picture of the two trucks-side by side with one going into combat, and the other coming out. It would illustrate what war could do to someone in just a week or two—the sad reality of war.

The troops going in were poised and ready. They were well-conditioned, well-fed, superbly trained, and highly motivated. Their equipment was new and in good working order. They were ready for combat.

The troops coming out were a stark contrast. Many had been wounded or shell-shocked. Their uniforms were filthy, ripped, torn, and covered in dirt, grease, food stains, and blood. They were exhausted, short on sleep, food, and medical attention. But all those images could be changed with a good shower, clean clothes, good food, needed sleep, and further medical treatment. What did not change were their eyes. It is said the eyes are the windows of one's soul, and looking into their eyes was what struck me and illustrated the horrors of war.

The eyes of the troops going in were bright and quick, darting from side-to-side. They may have been apprehensive and even shown signs of fear, but they were alert and sharp. The eyes of those coming out were dull, distant, not really focusing on anything. Some were affected by the morphine that had been pumped into their bodies, others were just exhausted, but all eyes were dull and unfocused. For many coming out, the war was over for them. They would return to the States; put this experience behind them, and move forward with jobs, marriage, children, and the everyday challenges and rewards that life offers. But for others, their war was not ending but just beginning. For a variety of reasons, some physical, others mental, the war was the catalyst for more pain and suffering. The trauma of what they had recently experienced would haunt them forever. Unable to hold on to jobs or marriages or family relationships, they would drift, endlessly lost in a pain that would not heal. Today, many are dead, but others continue to drift. Old men now, forgotten and lost.

These thoughts have grown for me with age. At the time, I was concerned solely for my job and my responsibility to my men. Trying to contemplate the deeper meanings of war while in the middle of one could get you killed. SSgt Ron taught me that lesson.

Graves Registration

During the Tet Offensive, we had units assigned to various positions and in support of numerous units. Vehicles went out to Hill 55, An Hoa, west to Hill 10, and large convoys north to Phu Bai and Hue. New troops were being added daily, others rotated out of the country, and it was a challenge to keep track of everyone. One small unit had been sent into Happy Valley and had engaged the enemy. The attack continued on and off into the night at Hill 10. The next day, our unit left Hill 10 and returned to our base camp. In the confusion of the attack, one new man was missing. It was believed that he had been wounded at Hill 10 and medevacked to the hospital at Danang. A call to the hospital was negative. Perhaps he was at Graves Registration, the building that served as a holding point for all killed in the division.

Since, as a new member assigned to our unit, he had not reported back from a mission, he may have been killed. That was the fear as no other units had reports of him. The executive officer, a major, called me in his office.

"Lieutenant, where is this man?" he screamed.

"I am not sure," I stammered.

"What? You must know where all your men are at all times. Get your ass over to Graves Registration and find out if he is there."

"Aye, aye, sir," I responded.

I had met the missing Marine, so I knew what he looked like and could make an identification.

Graves Registration was a long building near First Division headquarters. From the outside, it resembled any other supply building, gray with a tin roof. It looked like just another standard-looking building. But inside, it was entirely different. I walked in and stated I was there to identify a man assigned to my unit.

"Go through those doors, Lieutenant," I was told.

Despite the sweltering heat of the day, inside, it was very cold as I entered a large room. On steel tables were dead Marines being hosed off and being put into big refrigerators.

"Can I help you?" said the hose man. When I mentioned my mission, he motioned to another person sitting at a desk.

"Let's see what we have," said the Marine at the desk.

He was a little too cheerful, in my opinion, considering the situation. He proceeded to pull out trays and check the toe tags of dead bodies. There must have been 50 bodies filling up those refrigerators.

"I think this is your guy," he announced.

With that, the tray was pulled out, and I made the identification.

"Just sign here," he said. I did and left.

God, I hated the whole scene.

Guarding the Perimeter

I hesitate to mention this story because I do not want the reader to get the wrong idea. Despite what was said, there were no drugs and very little drinking in our companies. I cannot speak for other units or later, but when we went out on operations, everyone was clear-headed. That being said, we did have a few beers in the rear areas to ease the stress we were under continuingly.

I was partaking at the club, having just come off an operation and had not had anything to eat all day. I had a rule that all officers had to visit the perimeter during the night and talk with the troops. Perimeter duty is lonely, and having an officer show interest went a long way with troop morale. It was my turn at two AM to visit the troops. As I walked along the lines, the effects of my earlier indulgence were taking effect. By the time I reached the command bunker, I was a little dizzy.

The command bunker was 12 feet off the ground. One had to climb a ladder to get to the top. On top were radios and machine guns, along with three riflemen and two sergeants, all of whom were looking out at our forward perimeter. Below the bunker was rolls of concertina wire in rolls with razor-sharp edges—nasty stuff. I climbed the ladder and greeted the troops.

"How are things going?" I asked.

The young Marines fresh from Parris Island boot camp responded quickly. "Fine, Sir."

The sergeants further assured me everything was OK. With that assurance, I executed a very military about-face and prepared to climb down the ladder. However, in my state of confusion, I executed the about-face, took two steps, and marched right off the bunker!

What happened next was not good. I fell 12 feet into the concertina wire. I failed to mention that attached to the concertina wire was monofilament lines that went to trip flares. As I rolled around in the wire, I set off the damn flares. The whole perimeter lit up. Radios came to life.

"There is movement in Charlie Company lines, Charlie Company is being probed," echoed up and down the lines.

Even Division was alerted. Rifle bolts were slammed home as Marines were ready to shoot anything that moved. It is a miracle I was not shot. The young Marines were stunned. No amount of training had prepared them to see their commanding officer disappear off the top of a bunker. The sergeants pulled me out of the wire and told the troops it was a classified test.

The next day I had to report to the colonel.

"What the hell happened to you?" he demanded.

I was covered with scratches and cuts from the concertina wire. I couldn't very well say I had walked off a bunker. Before I could answer, the colonel accused me of being with prostitutes in the village. Considering the alternative, this was by far the best story. The colonel screamed at me for being a bad example.

"The only reason I am not writing you up is your combat record."

With that, the colonel shook his head, and I was dismissed.

SSgt Ron was very impressed.

Transitions

The Marines rotated back to the states every 13 months. Thus, it was time to say goodbye to SSgt Ron and Lt. Barry. In SSgt Ron's case, I drove him to the airport. He had his favorite tee shirt with him. It was a picture of a giant Marine with crisscrossing bandoleers. Underneath were the words: *"Yea though I walk through the valley of the shadow of death, I will fear no evil; cause I'm the meanest mother in the valley."*

He was a good platoon sergeant. The platoon functioned well under his unique leadership style. I appreciated his efforts and aggressive spirit. Yes, he was hard, but again some Marines required that discipline to keep them prepared for combat. A lot of Marines were alive because of his attention to detail and his demands for excellence.

As I stopped the jeep, we shook hands, and I told him to have fun. He smiled and asked if that was an order. I said it was.

"Well, Sir, then I will comply."

With that, he hopped out of the jeep and headed towards the plane. He had a swagger when he walked as if to say I am a Staff Sergeant in the United States Marine Corps. I want nothing more.

Some men are haunted by war. They think of the killings, confusion, politics, and sadness, leading them into dark areas where bad things can happen. Not SSgt Ron. Whether it was an enemy bunker or a bunk in a whorehouse, he attacked them with the same aggressive style and basked in the results. He was a dying breed.

A few days later, Lt. Barry and I sat on a sandbagged bunker looking out at Happy Valley.

"Just think Gris," said Lt. Barry, "In less than a week, I will be at Blacks Beach. I'll fire up a crooks and paddle the surfboard out to catch a smooth rolling wave. The California sun will be shining with a slight warm breeze, and I will be putting a few moves on the board as I head directly towards two nude models lying in the sand. And son, it doesn't get any better than that."

Who was I to argue with my commanding officer?

Captain Bob

The Battalion Commander had been keeping an eye on C Company. While we did our job, and there were no disciplinary actions of any kind, the Commander still felt it was time to tighten things up. Instead of selecting a Lieutenant that had been under the command of California Dreaming, he elected to take his Operations Officer, Captain Bob, and make him the Commanding Officer of C Company.

The change of Command ceremony had Lt. Barry presenting the guide arm (flag) to Captain Bob. Lt. Barry then stepped back waved to the troops like Richard Nixon leaving the White House for the last time and headed off to the California beaches. Captain Bob waited respectfully until Lt. Barry was out of range.

Then he issued his first order. "All officers and senior staff stand fast. All troops dismissed."

The troops dispersed quickly. Troops had a sixth sense about change, and they knew storm clouds were gathering. Captain Bob then gave his second order as he faced his officers and senior staff.

"In my office, NOW." A change had come to C Company.

Captain Bob had studied law in college, but rather than head to a desk job at legal, he had opted for combat. He was quick, smart, organized, and extremely knowledgeable. While he could be friendly, he was also very serious. His first order of business was to get the senior staff back in the war. The Marines rely more on their senior sergeants than other branches, and the good ones were the backbone of the Corps. The lazy ones put too much stress on junior staff and young officers.

Captain Bob would not allow that to happen. As he dictated his expectations, a senior staff sergeant pointed out some obscure regulations that would excuse senior staff from assignments. Under Lt. Barry, that would have been accepted. Not Captain Bob. He acknowledged that regulation and then quoted another that stated in the time of combat the Commanding Officer could supersede the previous regulations. The objection was dropped. Captain Bob knew all the regulations better than anyone.

It was now Captain Bob's turn to drill the officers. As we moved north, we traveled through different sectors, each with its own coordinates and call signs. There were mortars, artillery, infantry support, and air cover, and they had their own frequencies and call signs. Under Lt. Barry, we relied on the radio operations to take care of all frequencies and call signs, and we didn't bother to announce our presence as we entered different sectors. Captain Bob was not impressed. What happens if your radio operator is killed? If you are not announced in a sector, how will they recognize your unit?

These and many other questions were valid, and it was impossible to argue with Captain Bob. Immediately we got to work. Then there was accountability for your people. He would meet officers during the day and quiz them on where their troops were operating. You better have an answer. In short, Captain Bob was one of the most professional officers I had ever met, and he turned us into the number one company almost overnight.

Ambushed

Up until now, I had never really seen combat up close. Yes, I had been shot at and experienced both mortar and rocket attacks, but these had been reactions to hostile fire. While I wasn't complaining, I felt that maybe I had not done as much as others such as my friend Kel who was in constant contact with the enemy and Bear who was stationed along the dangerous demilitarized zone (DMZ) running convoys into Khe Sanh. I wondered how I would react. I was about to find out.

It was a typical day in the Nam. Hot, humid, a few scattered clouds. The assignment was quite simple. Take 12 trucks with supplies to an outpost northwest of Hill 10. Usually, a junior officer would take this assignment, but we were shorthanded, and this was a new location; so, I was selected.

I reviewed all the maps, supplies, security, equipment, and headed out of the compound into Happy Valley. After a couple of clicks, we turned north on a road we had not traveled before. As we moved along, there were plants and trees on each side as the road seemed to narrow more to a trail—still no problems as we proceeded. We came to a clearing with flat land on the right and large rice paddy on the left. There was a village to the left as well, but I did not pay much attention. One thing that caught my eye was there were no farmers in the rice paddies. But the Vietnamese had their own schedules, and I did not concern myself with their comings and goings.

We were three-quarters of the way across the rice paddy when the lead truck stopped causing the whole convoy to come to a halt. It was too narrow to pass. I immediately called out to the pace vehicle.

"Pace, why are we stopped?"

"There is a body across the road," was the answer from the pace driver. "Not sure if the person is dead or alive."

"Let's check it out," I said over the radio.

With that, I dismounted along with Rodriquez from security, and together we were joined by a platoon sergeant from another vehicle. We moved forward. Perhaps it was an NVA soldier as they were known to leave their wounded. We were near the second vehicle when there was a massive explosion. All I recall was the noise, rocks, dirt, and pieces of metal flying everywhere. The concussion blew me into the rice paddy. I may have been out for a few seconds-not sure. Dazed and unable to hear anything, I crawled back to the road. Rodriquez was lying off to the side with what medics would describe as a sucking chest wound. Shrapnel had pierced his chest, and his aorta was pumping blood, spurting like a fountain. Rodriquez, like most Hispanics, was Catholic, and he had rosary beads around his neck. He clutched them with his right hand and was praying:

"Hail Mary, full of grace," as I approached.

Another Marine put his hand on Rodriquez's chest. His hand was red with blood. The platoon sergeant was in a ditch, and I noticed his foot was not right. Instead of pointing forward, it was pointed backward, his leg was shattered and twisted. He had taken his belt off and tightened it above his right knee as a tourniquet. He was mumbling orders and appeared to be going into shock.

As I realized the extent of injuries to my men, the village opened up with AK 47 fire. In an instant, I knew what happened. Someone had laid out a body knowing we would stop. They waited until a group of us was near the lead truck and crossed two wires: setting off the mine. Then they opened fire; we were caught in an ambush.

My men reacted quickly, returning fire both to the village and in the rice paddy where other enemy soldiers were firing. There were red lines everywhere as our machine guns tracers were visible. Tracers were every fifth round, which was red-tipped. When all you saw looked like a continuous red line, it represented a massive number of bullets being directed on the enemy. We could hold our own, but we were exposed, and they were dug in hiding behind the huts and fences of the village.

"Lieutenant," screamed a Marine, "Do something, or we will lose Rodriquez." I immediately called back to our headquarters, switched to the medical channel, and called for a medevac.

I had to save my men.

We continued to return fire. Suddenly, I heard the medevac chopper, "Charlie Six (my call sign), Charlie Six, this in Med One over."

"Med One I copy," I answered.

"LZ (landing zone) too hot- cannot land."

Now, what would I do? No Medevac and no infantry close enough to help. Fear can be crippling. But then something happened to me. What the Marines counted on and what they trained me for. Fear gave way to anger. The same anger that had challenged the recruiter, the same anger that I found in pugil stick fights, the same anger that gave me the ability to climb up those hills in the mud and rain. I would not let these bastards kill my men. I screamed at the radio operator:

"Get me air!"

The radio operator quickly dialed up the air frequency and handed the phone to me "Playboy, Playboy, this is Charlie

Six, over," I yelled into the phone over the firing of our weapons and bullets whizzing around us.

You had to love the air wing and their colorful call signs. After some time, "This is Playboy leader one, over," came the reply.

"Roger, one, this is Charlie Six, need close air support. We are under fire at coordinates," and I checked my map, hoping I was getting them down as all were coded.

"We copy, will take a look, Playboy Leader out," came the reply.

The radio went dead. We continued to fire, and I screamed at my men to practice fire discipline as I did not want to run out of ammo. I was screaming at every one since I could not hear from the ringing in my ears. Then, the radio came alive.

"Charlie six, we have your Pos (position) and are on approach. Stay low, Charlie Six."

After what seemed like a minute or two, it sounded like a low rumble from a train pulling into a railroad station. The rumbling grew louder and louder and became a deafening roar, the ground seems to shake, and suddenly two Marine jets roared in. I would guess about one hundred feet off the ground. They flashed by in an instant and shot straight up and split off in a V, disappearing into the clouds. They were gone. Perhaps a few seconds went by-again, it is hard to remember, I was pretty dazed. Then the village and the rice paddy exploded in a ball of orange and black fire. Canisters of napalm (jellied gasoline) exploded. There was no more firing. The village was destroyed.

The troops cheered, but I had no time to waste. I called again for the medevac, and this time they responded. Within five minutes, the medevac helicopter landed on the ground to my right, and the tail door dropped open.

"Over here," I yelled at the Navy corpsmen who were running to us.

By this time, Rodriquez was ash white, and his eyes were closing. He still clutched the rosary beads in his right hand, but his left hand hung limp.

"Please save him," I implored to the corpsmen, "He is a good kid." The corpsman put two fingers on his neck, feeling for a pulse, checked his body, and shook his head.

"He's done, we can't save him," he said and literally tossed him aside.

In combat, you practice medical triage. Save those you can and do not spend time on those you can't.

"We can save these two," as he ran to the sergeant and another Marine that had been hit during the firefight.

They carried the two injured Marines into the chopper, and two others jumped in. They had been shot, but their wounds were not too serious. Nevertheless, some wounds in the rice paddies led to serious infections, and it was good to get them treated with antibiotics. Then Rodriquez's body was thrown in the chopper.

"How about you," said the corpsman looking at me.

I had some cuts on my arms.

"I am staying with my men," I said.

I was not really hurt except I could hardly hear.

"Suit yourself," said the Corpsmen.

They took off. The four Marines were taken to a hospital center in Danang and would be operated on. One would lose his leg, and another would never play sports again, but all survived. Rodriquez would go to graves registration.

There was no time to reflect on what had happened. The blown truck was picked up, and we moved on to the outpost and delivered our supplies. Since it took longer than expected, we would spend the night in the field and return to base the next day. That night, the men talked quietly. Rodriquez was well-liked, but combat did not allow for too much emotion. Rather, the men cleaned their weapons, checked equipment, and reflected on winning the firefight. As for me, I thought about the airstrike. We killed a lot of people. Most were enemies, but some were just innocent villagers. On the other hand, if I had not called in the strike, more Marines would have died, perhaps all of us. To this day, I have never doubted my decision.

My other thought was for Rodriquez. There was no military order on how we proceeded forward that day. Rodriquez was to my left, maybe five feet away. It just as easily could have been reversed. Then it would be Rodriquez reflecting on the event, and I would be at graves registration. Someone would be hosing me down, putting me into one of those freezers. Later, my body would be placed in a silver casket and flown to California and later across the country to Delaware or perhaps Massachusetts. Somewhere an American flag would be put on the casket, a hearse would pick it up, and deliver it to my mother.

Just five feet.

R&R-Rest and Recuperation

After my close call in the ambush and because I had been in the Nam for over eight months, I was up for Rest and Recuperation. R&R was the military's answer to being in a combat zone 24/7. Each man was allowed one week to visit a location of choice out of the country. There were eight choices. Hawaii was first for the married men who would meet their wives or soon to be wives. Other spots included Bangkok, Tokyo, and Australia. I chose Australia.

As with everything else in the war, it was a strange setting. Military personnel from several units, all in utility uniforms, stepped on a commercial jet at Danang. From being in a war zone one minute, we were now up in the friendly skies headed to Australia. After flying over the Pacific region, we landed in Darwin, Australia, for refueling. Then back in the skies and on to Sydney.

When we arrived at the airport, officials entered the plane and sprayed disinfectant all through the plane as if we were diseased cattle. Everyone was too excited to get too upset. We were loaded on buses and driven to the airport hotels. It was very pleasant, and my hotel was nice. Not overly fancy but a thousand times better than Danang or Kin Village. For me, there were priorities for R&R.

The first one probably would not come to mind, but it was a shower. I had not had a warm shower in over eight months. Yes, there were showers at the base camp, but they were cold, and with limited water, you simply got wet, soaped up, rinsed off, and got out. Others were waiting, and perhaps it lasted two minutes. I had those showers maybe twice a month. This was just like home. I must have stood in that warm shower for half an hour. Never has a shower felt better.

The second thing on my list was to call my mother. We had written many letters back and forth, and I knew she wanted to hear my voice. With help from a radio operator somewhere in the world, the call was put through to my hometown. It was great to hear her voice. We spent time catching up- on how things were going back in the world. We called the States "the world" as we felt we were living in a sixteenth-century time-capsule in the Nam. For my part, I told her everything was fine, and I was in no danger.

"It's all routine. Just resupplying units. Most of my time is in the safety of the base camp," I said. There was no need to worry her. I know she knew differently, but why go into details.

Now on to the third item of business. The Australians had arranged for all of us to go to parties at various hotels around the city. We had brought along some civilian clothes to look civilianized – except for our noticeably short haircuts. Anyways, we entered the hotel, and to our pleasant surprise, there were hundreds of Australian girls. The mini skirt fad had hit Australia, and the girls were beautiful in the shortest dresses I had ever seen. Keep in mind, we had been in the jungles, and the bar was not too high. However, I thought they were all gorgeous.

I went up to one that I thought was cute and started talking. She said she wanted to show me around the city. In one of the great pick-up lines of all time, I said I wanted to show her my room. She laughed and said that would be fine. I never got to see much of the city. I can remember back home when family members would quiz me about the sights of Australia, I would just smile and say I did not see too many of them.

Time went by quickly, and soon we were back on a plane and back in the war. It was so hard to comprehend being in combat, jerked out for a time of fun and good living, and then right back in the war. It took some adjustments, but you really could not afford to give it too much thought and still do your job.

Company Commander

It was time for Captain Bob to rotate back to the states. I approached him in his office and shook his hand. "I want to thank you for all you taught me," I said. "I learned a lot from you."

"I hope so," said Captain Bob, "Because I have recommended you to be the next Company Commander."

Company Commander is an honor. The colonel makes the decision, and he had many options to choose from. He could take one of our four platoon commanders, or he could take any of his staff officers. All of them would rather command a company than be stuck in some thankless staff position. Or he could go to another company and take any of their officers. I was honored that he selected me.

As a young platoon commander, I had avoided the spotlight as much as possible. I was like Ensign Pulver, the shy officer played by Jack Lemon in *Mister Roberts*. But as a Company Commander, I was very visible. Each day the Battalion Commander, a lieutenant colonel, would meet us in his office. The executive officer would be on his right, followed by all the staff officers representing logistics, operations, intelligence, and personnel. All the company officers would be to the left. The colonel was a wise leader. He would always ask for our opinions and would take them into consideration. Usually, the next day after considering our suggestions, he would issue the orders and turn to the executive officer, a major, to see they were carried out. The major was a large man with a face like a bulldog and a personality to match. He loved to chew out lieutenants, and we all tried to avoid displeasing him.

"Don't piss off the Bulldog," was the first bit of advice I got before my first meeting.

Thanks to Captain Bob, all I really had to do was keep his policies and programs in place and work through my sergeants as Sergeant Tom had taught me back at Camp Lejeune. The result was we had a great company. One problem, however, was maintenance. Equipment was breaking down. I needed a top-notch maintenance man. Delta company had the best, but he drank too much and, therefore, was not held in high regard. One night I traded some equipment and a couple of troops to Delta company for their maintenance sergeant. Delta Company CO was happy to get rid of him. His name was Sergeant Jenkins. I told Sergeant Jenkins he could have two days off a week. I did not care where he went or what he did. In return, I expected the equipment to be the best in the Battalion. Sergeant Jenkins liked the idea. Of course, it was totally against any form of military regulations to let someone wander off for two days. Still, I had learned from SSgt Ron that some flexibility worked well. As a result, we had the best maintenance of any company. The colonel thought I was a mechanical genius.

New Officers

As the Company Commander, I now oversaw the training and actions of four platoon commanders. They would report directly to me and command their four platoons. The relationship between the platoon sergeants and the new lieutenants was extremely important. In theory, lieutenants would have more education and be better equipped to handle tactics, concepts, and unusual circumstances. The sergeants would offer firsthand experience and an ability to handle the troops. If they came together and merged those talents, it would produce a bond and a well-functioning platoon. Most of the time, it did. But not always.

Despite warnings during officer training, some lieutenants would allow their rank and their superior education to avoid listening to the experienced sergeants. This would be a problem as the sergeants were skilled at being respectful, and at the same time, enjoyed watching the new lieutenants get into trouble if they pulled rank. I watched the relationships between the new lieutenants and the sergeants very closely. One time things did not go well.

The assignment was simple. A new artillery unit had moved into our sector, and I wanted to be sure we were together on call signs and operational procedures. Today, the contact would be accomplished by phones. Still, our phones were somewhat unreliable, as there were hills between our units and theirs. Also, discussing call signs over the air was dangerous, so I dispatched a new lieutenant who had graduated from a very well-known college in the east. He had just joined our outfit, and I told him to take a jeep along with a sergeant and drive up Highway One to the new unit. It was a good assignment for a new officer as it would allow him to take responsibility, become familiar with the important call signs, and allow him to learn the area from an experienced sergeant who had been in the country longer. I expected the mission to be accomplished and both men back in the compound by 11AM.

To my great surprise, they returned by 9:30. The sergeant did not look so well.

"How did you make it back so quickly?" I asked.

"Well, we did not wait for the mine sweep," stated an incredibly angry sergeant.

"What?!" I said in astonishment.

"I did not see the need to wait," said the very book smart officer.

"Sergeant, that will be all, you are dismissed," I said. I paused to let the sergeant leave. "Are you telling me, lieutenant, you went down the road in a jeep before the road was swept for mines? Are you crazy? Do you have any idea how dangerous that was?"

"Well, there have not been any mines recently," was the answer.

Now I was really getting mad.

"Let me tell you something. Some time ago, a jeep of ours hit an anti-tank mine. I saw that jeep, and you could not tell the front from the back; it was that mangled. And you know what, if you looked on the inner sides of the twisted metal, it looks like someone threw a pizza at it; all different colors sticking to the metal. Only it was skin, blood, body fluids, and pieces of cloth from two Marines. The patrol that found the jeep put as many body parts as they could find into one body bag, and it took forensics to make the positive identifications. That could have been you and your driver. I would have to write the letters back home to your families, telling them some made-up story of enemy involvements because I could not tell the truth. The truth is for all your education, you must be the stupidest officer I ever met. Losing you would be one thing, but I would lose a good sergeant as well as a jeep, which is hard to replace. Lieutenant, if you ever fail to follow the procedure again, I will have you up on charges; is that clear?"

He acknowledged it was in a rather embarrassed tone.

I knew I had made my point. He had the potential to be a good officer, but this is how bad things happened in the Nam. The routine led to carelessness, and by shortcutting procedures, you could make a mistake that would cost a life. It required constant discipline to avoid tragic mistakes. Time after time, I would preach that to my men.

"It only takes one mistake to lose a life. Never let your guard down. Always be alert.

Our goal is to complete our missions and go home in one piece."

Farewell to the Nam

As a Company Commander, I spent less time in the field and more time overseeing the operations of the company. I did go out on convoys and once was nearly killed by one of my own men. It happened when my driver, upon receiving sniper fire, ran our jeep into a ditch, grabbed his M-16, spun around, and starting firing inches from my face. I got powder burns from the incident. We laughed about it later.

Unfortunately, not all incidents were funny. Men do die. While on patrol, two of my men were killed in an ambush, another by a sniper, and another by a rocket attack. I was not present when these events happened. As their Commanding Officer, I had to write letters to their families, and I truly hated that task. The Department of Defense would send the official letter, and it would always be delivered by two Marines. But I felt I owed it to the families to write a more personal note. Some officers simply copied a recommended letter, but I felt it should represent a more personal touch. I did my best to find the words that I hoped would offer some comfort.

I had less than a month to go when the major called me on the phone. "The colonel is about to rotate out, and he wants to see you," said the major.

"What does he want to see me for, major?" I asked.

"Just report in at 1400, Lieutenant. I do not have to give a reason," said the bulldog Major.

"Yes, sir."

At exactly 1400, I stood at attention before the colonel's desk.

"Lieutenant Griswold reporting as ordered, sir," I said in my most military voice.

"At ease, Lieutenant," said the colonel. "I will be leaving soon, and I want you to know I am putting you in for some awards. You have done a good job."

"Thank you, sir," I responded.

I was always a little uncomfortable about awards. They were so subjective. Some senior officers felt everyone who served in combat should get an award. Others felt you had to fight off at least five enemy soldiers in hand to hand combat to get an award. Then any award had to go through channels and be reviewed. That process was also subjective, and awards could be lowered or even rejected. I had heard of men, especially officers, getting awards under questionable circumstances. I knew men who should have gotten awards and got nothing. It was a flawed system.

The colonel continued, "First, the Purple Heart." The Purple Heart is given to those who had been killed or injured in combat.

Again, it could be subjective. Death or being seriously wounded was obvious, but there were gray areas. Technically, I had cut my arm from either shrapnel or perhaps a flying piece of rock or glass during the ambush, and it did bleed. I had spilled blood in a combat zone as a direct result of enemy action. But it was such a small cut. I had been hurt worse falling off my bike and being kicked in soccer, elbowed in basketball, and getting hit with baseballs. But far more important to me was the fact that others that day had been killed and hurt very badly. To me, it would cheapen the award for me to accept it.

"Colonel, I cannot accept the award," I said.

"Why not, you were hurt."

I gave him my thoughts. "Further colonel, one of my men in the group the evening of the attack asked me if I was putting in for a Purple Heart. I said no, and the men nodded their heads in approval.

They respected my answer, and if I accepted the award, I would be going back on my word."

The colonel listened, and he smiled. "Very well, I will not put you in for the Purple Heart. But I am putting you in for the Bronze Star."

"Really, gosh, the Bronze Star," I answered. I was surprised. In the Marines, it represented a high honor of valor.

"Colonel, I am not sure I deserve it."

"Lieutenant, your actions saved a lot of lives and brought destruction to the enemy. It more than qualifies."

"But Colonel, there were so many who contributed that day. There were the radio operators, the men at the division that reviewed and approved the actions, the air traffic controls, the pilots who flew the mission, the corpsmen, the helicopter pilots, and most of all my brave men who acted as trained and returned fire to keep the enemy at bay. Without them, we would have been overrun, and all of us killed. They are just as deserving as I am."

"Well, Lieutenant, I cannot give the medal to everyone. You were in command, and it was your leadership that was responsible."

"Colonel- "

"That's enough, Lieutenant. I will agree not to put you in for the Purple Heart, but you are being put in for the Bronze Star. You are dismissed."

I snapped to attention, took one step back, said, "Aye, Aye Sir," and left his office.

Outside, I still felt I was undeserving, but at the same time, I was thinking about my Dad. I smiled and looked towards the heavens. I had struggled in so many ways and never quite succeeded in what had been expected. But to command United States Marines and to be written up for one of their highest awards was something I feel would have made him proud. It was a particularly good feeling.

My tour was up. I had spent 13 months in Vietnam less the week of screwing up embarkation school. I was ready to go home. On my last day, a formation was held, and I presented the guide arm to the new company commander. He was an exceptionally good officer over from Bravo company. I knew he would do well. I thanked the troops for all their support and was ready to dismiss the company when the first sergeant approached.

"Lieutenant, the men wanted you to have this gift."

This was unusual, especially in Nam, where often there was division, if not an actual dislike between the troops and the officers. It was a small black box. I opened it, and it was a beautiful watch. I was overcome with emotions. These Marines had so little. The few dollars they made went back home to their families. To think that they would take some of that needed money and purchase a gift meant so much. I thanked them and felt a lump building in my throat. I could not show any emotion; that would not be good. What could I say? Then in an instant, I found the right words.

"Knowing all of you, I am sure it was stolen."

It was the perfect touch. The company exploded in laughter. When the laughter died down, I told them I would always treasure the watch; and I have. It meant more to me than the medals that would follow. Upon receiving the watch and thanking the men, I did an about-face and marched out of the Nam.

Welcome Home

Arrival

I heard stories of plane trips back to the states where troops were yelling, screaming, celebrating with drinks, and harassing the stewardess. But on my flight with combat Marines, no one said anything. You could have heard a pin drop. Sometimes there would be an occasional sob or choking as someone thought of a close buddy left behind. For me, I just stared out the window at the endless water, grateful to God for being on that flight.

Arriving in California, we entered a commercial terminal. We had heard stories of service members being harassed and even spit on. This was discussed as the men were getting ready to depart the plane.

"I dare one of them to challenge me," was said by most. This group was ready for a fight. Considering we were hardened by endless patrols up and down mountains and slogging through rice paddies, it would not have been much of a fight against any protestors.

For me, there was a bad feeling and very mixed emotions. Among Marines, we had discussed the war and the tactics employed, and many felt the war should have been fought differently. Most favored a more aggressive approach where we would take the fight to the enemy, but some felt we should not have even been there. But that was between us. For outsiders to take out their frustrations on the military was quite different. Who were they to challenge our role? We had done what was asked, and we had been the ones who endured the lousy weather and a determined enemy. Despite differences in strategies, we had closed ranks on those attacking us. I was as mad as anyone in the group.

Yet, as one of the officers in charge, controlling my emotions was important. If a fight broke out, how would I handle it? Would I try to stop it, or would I participate? I was not a hundred percent sure, and it was unsettling.

Fortunately, nothing happened. As we walked through the terminal to get our bags, most Marines had their fists clenched, but there was no need. We got a few dirty looks, but no threatening gestures, and definitely no one came close to spitting on us. There was no welcome home, or thanks for your service, but no incidents. Most just looked away, not wanting to associate with us. Under the circumstances that was fine by me, but I must admit it was a little disheartening to think of so many who had given their lives or been badly wounded; the best we could hope for was to be ignored.

I caught a ride on a military transport plane to a Marine Air Base and flew across country landing just north of Philadelphia. The plan was to take the train from Philly to New York and a ride to Connecticut to meet my family. Since I had a couple of hours to kill, I walked into a Philadelphia bar around the corner from the train station. Being in uniform, I noticed people moved away from me. No one wanted to speak with a military person. Then a man approached. Middle-aged, he resembled Archie Bunker from *All in the Family*.

He asked, "You're in the Marines, right?"

"Yes," I said.

"Well," he said, "I was in WW II, 5th Marine Division, Iwo Jima." I was immediately impressed and welcomed the opportunity to share a few war stories. I stuck out my hand and said the universal Marine greeting,

"Semper Fi."

The man did not take my hand. He looked hard at me and said, "We won our war, what happened to you?"

I was stunned. I started to explain that this was different. The goal was not so much to win as to hold ground for the South Vietnamese. I tried to explain how Laos and Cambodia were sanctuaries, and it was hard to win under those conditions. He was unimpressed.

"Marines win wars," he countered.

I had nothing further to say. I put down my drink and walked out.

I passed the train station and headed down by the river. There was a park, and I walked in and sat on a bench. It was dark, and I was alone. My head was a kaleidoscope of thoughts. It seemed everyone was mad at me for my service, and I was caught in some type of crossfire. The hawks were mad because we did not produce more defined victories, and the doves hated us for being there. Then a Marine, a brother in arms, a hero from Iwo Jima, and someone I looked up to held me in utter contempt. Even worse were the casualties from my Basic School class. Word had filtered back on those who had been killed. Dale, Charlie, Steve, Norman, Harold, John, and many others. They were brave Marine officers who died, leading their troops often outnumbered against enemy forces. Then there was Rodriquez, and the letters I had to write. At that moment, something happened that had not happened in 13 months. I started to cry. I tried to stop. But I couldn't. I just couldn't.

Parties

I pulled myself together, caught the next train, and arrived in New York City as planned. I got a ride to Connecticut, and it was close to midnight when we pulled into the Taft Hotel in New Haven. There to greet me was my mother and her two brothers, Franklin and Boyne, who had come from New Orleans and Cincinnati, to welcome me home. It was so nice of them to come from that far away. I was very grateful. I hugged my Mom, shook hands with them, and we ventured into the Tap Room at the Taft for a few drinks. My uncles had both been in World War II, and they understood I had no real interest in talking about war. Instead, they brought me up to speed on family events. It was great to catch up. As for my Mom, she just smiled and threw back a few bourbons; happy her son had survived.

Back home, I remember how good it was just to be in my own room. As I looked at my bed, I realized I did not have to put my boots, helmet, and weapons in a line. I did not have to worry about sirens or gunfire or think about coordinates or fields of fire. For the first time in a year, I could just sleep.

I slept till noon and then went downstairs to have breakfast. Mom was waiting.

"What do you want?" she asked.

"A Bloody Mary sounds good."

No problem, mother was an excellent bartender. After we talked for a while, she announced we would have a party to welcome me home. Mom was much like *Auntie Mame,* who was known for throwing parties in the Broadway musical. Back in Kentucky, my mother had majored in parties and could throw a party at a moment's notice.

In a few days, guests started arriving for the welcome home party. Most of the Griswold's had on their Ivy league Yale jackets with the gray slacks of fall replacing the white slacks of summer. The ladies were in fashionable dresses. I was in uniform, and in the words of Colonel Pickering from *My Fair Lady*, "It was a grand occasion." Everyone shook my hands and offered appreciation for my efforts, and I thanked everyone. After some small talk, one of my older cousins, who had been President of a large corporation, held up his hand and asked for quiet.

"David, tell us what's going on with this Viet Nam thing?" he queried.

Everyone went silent and looked at me. I was unprepared to say anything, and at that moment, I felt as if I was being asked to give the annual report at General Motors.

I started off by saying I was just a lieutenant and not privileged to strategies at higher levels. That seemed to be disappointing to the group, but I continued. I explained the sanctuaries and how it was difficult to win the war under these circumstances. I said it was complicated. At the mention of complicated, I could see I was losing my audience. Mercifully, my cousin held up his hand.

"Well, David, we are glad you made it back. Let's have a toast."

Everyone relaxed raised their glasses, and I was off the hook. At that point, people drifted into groups to discuss the concerns of the day. There was a rumor the chef at the club might be leaving, and that just could not happen. After all, nobody could make a Lobster Newburg like the chef. Then the new minister had delivered a sermon that had raised eyes brows and that had to be addressed. But of most concern were moles on the golf course. Why just last week, Henry

Wadsworth III had lost a birdie on the fourteenth hole when his ball was deflected by a molehill.

At that point, I thought I was going mad. I wanted to scream that men were dying in Vietnam, and nobody cared about moles. The other side of my brain told me to relax. After all, it wasn't these people who were in charge. They were important people conditioned to making important decisions. But the war was so confusing to them as it was to everyone. They wanted to support the military and had little use for the protestors. Still, on the other hand, they were increasingly skeptical of a government that kept promising victories with little to show for the effort. Unable to form a firm opinion, they turned to things they could control. With a small war going on in my head, I headed into the kitchen to consult with Professor Jim Beam from a fine family in Kentucky. It was at this point I felt a soft hand on my shoulder.

"Are you alright?" my mother asked.

"I guess I am just tired," I said.

"Well, you need to rejoin the party; everyone wants to see you."

"Sure, Mom," I could never say no to her.

I rejoined the party and drifted from group to group smiling and nodding my head at the conversations. Jim Beam had calmed the warring factions in my brain, and to be honest, things became a little vague. I do remember saying I thought some C4 could fix the mole problem. My cousin, who undoubtedly thought C 4 was some type of weed killer, thought it was a splendid idea. C 4 is a high-density explosive that we used to blow up enemy bunkers. A pound of C 4 would have obliterated the fourteenth green. Still, I am fairly sure it would have eradicated the mole problem. I wonder what old Henry Wadsworth would say as he came over the crest of the hill and saw a smoldering crater where his beloved green had been. It would have been a scene right out of the comedy movie *Caddy Shack*. And so, there I was grinning like an idiot while eight thousand miles away, Blue Lights, Scout, and Tex were slogging through the rice paddies on another endless patrol.

A few weeks later, another party was planned. This would be my three college roommates, wives, and friends who had been with me when I was inducted into the Marines. What a difference a year makes. From carefree college guys, the war had divided them. One was for it, one against, and one indifferent. The evening began with a few beers and some pizza. The talk centered around our college days and all the good times. It seemed so innocent in comparison to what was happening at this moment. My roommates talked about their children. Rick had a little girl, Skip had a boy, and Jim and his wife were expecting. I did not have too much to contribute. The party was to welcome me back, but talking about the war was difficult. I did not want to come across as too military and make them feel uneasy. Perhaps some felt uncomfortable since they had not served. Outside of we are glad you made it back, not much was said. We just reminisced about college days.

Then around eleven in the evening, it happened. Someone, I really do not remember who lit up a marijuana cigarette. Seeing someone light up a joint encouraged a few others to join in. Almost insistently, two groups were formed. From my perspective, it was far more than smoking pot. It was a form of rebellion. And much of that rebellion was against us- the military. This illegal act was an attack on my military friends and me, some of whom had been killed. I am sure that was not the intent of the smokers, but that was my take.

Words were exchanged.

"We would be winning the war if we had more support at home," said someone in my group.

"The war is stupid, and we have no business being there," countered the other side.

I was trying to remain calm, but I was far from happy.

Then someone in the other group, I have no idea which as I had had a lot to drink, said. "I don't see the problem with burning the flag."

"What did you say," I shouted.

"Well, it just a piece of cloth, and it stands for the injustices we are carrying out."

All I could think of was the hilltops where the flag flew, and we stood in silence as prayers were offered for fallen Marines. I was trembling with rage and moving closer to a real fight.

Once again, it was Skip, the golfer, who stepped in. "Hey Gris, forget about them. Think about that hot date of yours."

"What," I answered.

"Your hot date. Why I might move on her myself," Skip said with his typical grin.

"But you're married," I smiled.

"Yes, but not necessarily at this moment."

I started to laugh, and any confrontation was avoided. I am not sure anyone else could have had the same effect on me. Skip was one of a kind. My anger passed, but the divisiveness was so indicative of the times.

The next day we said our goodbyes, but it was tense. It would be ten years before any future reunions would even be considered. Today, time has smoothed over the wounds, but the scars remain. We are all friends and get together each year to play golf. We always have a great time, and I am grateful for their friendships, but the war is never discussed. Never.

Adjusting to the States

California Duty

I reported back to the Marines for my last year of service. It passed quickly with nothing too noteworthy from a military perspective. After the intensity of Nam, everything seemed routine. I was promoted to Captain, which is fast for three years in service. I would like to think it was because of my combat record. Still, in truth, so many Marine Lieutenants and Captains were killed in Nam that rank moved quickly, and almost everyone in my timeslot was promoted.

Often, I was asked about my thoughts and feelings about the war once I returned. I really did not give it too much thought. I was grateful, of course, for being spared, but I did not get too involved in the political battles. I simply committed myself to my next assignment and to be a good officer for my men. That would produce challenges of a different nature.

My duty station was in California. I was assigned to the Third Marine Air Wing at El Toro just south of Los Angeles. I had several duties as we supported base operations.

But my main job was to try and keep my troops out of trouble. It was 1969, and America had exploded into craziness, and the capital of crazy land was Southern California.

Protest of the war and racial tensions were everyday events. When mixed with an abundance of alcohol, drugs, free love, and an anything-goes attitude, you had a dangerous situation. My troops were victims of these times.

Psychiatrists have written about wars and the need for men to decompress after combat. That happened in WW II as the war was over, and the troops came home with a week of decompressing aboard troopships. Further, they were met with cheering crowds and marching bands. Korea was not the same, but it was manageable. But nothing in America's military history compared to the Nam. Shot at one day, the troops found themselves deposited in Southern California the next. There were no marching bands, and many knew that in one year, they would be headed back to a war that was not being won. These combinations of events produced a "What the hell' kind of attitude.

At the base, the troops were fine. They did their jobs and maintained good military discipline but, off the base in crazy land was a different matter. Almost daily, I stood in front of a Major who wanted answers to the latest transgressions my men had committed. In fact, pulling Marines out of jail for fighting and consulting them on why they were four months behind on their car payments was so common that I assigned the actions to a junior lieutenant.

Two instances called out for my attention and demonstrated how crazy the times were. "Captain," said the major, "We have a problem with Private Jefferson."

"What would that be, sir?"

"Well, he is being charged with bigamy."

"Bigamy?"

"That's right, Captain, he was married last week in Tijuana. Normally that would be OK, but Private Jefferson already has a wife, and this is not Saudi Arabia. It seems the US has laws that frown on a collection of wives."

An hour later, Private Jefferson was standing in front of my desk. "Private Jefferson, did you get married last week in Tijuana?" I asked.

"You mean to that little girl at the bar?"

"Yes"

"Well, come on, Captain. She said I would have to marry her to sleep with her, and I was pretty drunk, and I never thought it was for real, and besides Captain, Mexico is a foreign country, so it doesn't count, right?"

"Wrong Private, I am afraid it does count."

The grin was gone. "Gosh, Captain, my wife is not going to like this."

"I am guessing she won't."

Another incident involved one of my best sergeants. The major informed me he was at the base hospital and in bad shape. I immediately went to see him. He had returned from the siege at Khe Sanh and had earned numerous medals for his actions under constant enemy fire. Now he was in serious condition in a base hospital.

"Sergeant, what happened?" I asked. The entire size of his head was black and blue, and he was groggy from pain medication.

"Well, Captain, my wife hit me with a cast-iron skillet."

I immediately wondered if it was a Griswold skillet. "Why did she do that?" I uttered in amazement.

"Well, um, err, she um came home early-"

"And"

"Well, I had my girlfriend over, and we were in bed, and my wife was apparently upset and-"

"What," I yelled, "you brought your girlfriend to your home?"

"I guess that was not a good idea, huh?"

Growing up in Connecticut, attending prep school, college, and even basic training had not prepared me for anything like this. It was about to get even crazier.

My commanding officer, a lieutenant colonel, was a dedicated Marine who had distinguished himself as a pilot.

However, his views of his troops were far more laid back than what I had experienced in the Nam. He was very friendly and was always willing to do nice things for "his boys." The great fishing trip was a prime example.

The colonel called another officer and me into his office. "You know what we need for good morale?" asked the colonel.

"A beach party?" I volunteered. I always liked beaches.

"No," said the colonel," Everyone does that. Many of our fellows have never been deep sea fishing. They will be getting out soon to return to the middle of our country. They will never have experienced the joy of catching a large saltwater fish. We should have a deep-sea fishing trip!" he declared

I looked at the other officer in the room in disbelief.

"Colonel, you want us to take twenty-five Marines out in the ocean on a fishing trip?" I tentatively asked.

"Exactly, Captain. It will be a great experience for them. Oh, and be sure and get some beers for the troops."

"But sir, understand these Marines have all come out of intense combat, and their idea of a good time may exceed regulations," I warned.

"No, buts Captain, make it happen." With that command, he concluded the meeting and went off to his scheduled tee time at the golf course.

"Has he lost his mind," my fellow officer laughed. "You are going to take a boatload of Marines fresh out of the Nam out fishing in the hot sun with cases of beer? Has the Coast Guard been informed?"

"It should be interesting," I offered.

We assembled at the fishing pier at five-thirty in the morning. The troops were fired up. Since the colonel had approved drinking for the trip, the Marines showed their commitment to the cause by bringing vodka, gin, and a variety of whiskeys aboard to add some more inspiration to the festive occasion. Shots and beers were the order of the day. By the time the boat got underway, half the group was on their way to getting really hammered, and the rest were not far behind.

As we headed to the fishing grounds and land faded away, I felt I was on a voyage of the damned. The boat trip lasted about an hour when the captain of the vessel said we were on the fishing grounds, and the first mate would be instructing us on the proper way to bait the hooks and fish off the sides. Fishing off a large boat with 25 people requires some attention to detail. The troops were far past that point. Almost immediately, lines were tangled, and tempers grew short. Some of the troops took fishing seriously and were upset with the others who could have cared less.

"You're not doing this right," said one conscientious Marine.

"So, what, are they going to send me back to Nam for fishing wrong?" laughed another.

Upset with the instructions from the first mate and fishing in general, a few threw their rods and reels overboard. They went back to serious drinking and heated discussion on how they fought the enemy back in Nam.

Others did catch fish and thought it great fun to throw fish at other Marines. One Marine fell in the fish well. The first mate instructed a Marine on better ways to fish, and the Marine instructed the first mate that he would throw him overboard if he didn't shut up. The first mate disappeared below decks and was not seen for the remainder of the trip.

In short, it was a disaster. By noon, the entire group was drunk and falling all over the place, with charges being brought by everyone against everyone. Corporals were going to write up privates and sergeants were going to write up corporals, and the captain of the vessel was concerned for his boat and the safety of his crew. He felt the need to call for assistance on the radio.

Normally officers would have put an immediate stop to such undisciplined activity. But this was not a controlled environment. The colonel had sanctioned the trip, and most of the Marines were getting out shortly. They had impressive combat records, and writing them up on charges would be hard to support. I, too, was about to transfer out, and the last thing I wanted was to have my transfer extended in multiple strings of court-martials. Plus, I was the ranking officer, and this would not look good on my record. The best thing to do was to simply disengage.

I suggested to the captain that perhaps it was in the best interest of his boat, equipment, and crew to head back to shore. The captain enthusiastically agreed. We motored back to port and arrived at the dock. Some Marines jumped into the water, others were throwing up over the side while a few others thought it great fun to throw fish at the folks on the dock. It was not exactly what one would see on a Marine recruiting poster.

We were met by the colonel who had ventured down to the docks to greet "his boys."

With a very quick look, the colonel deemed it a great success and rapidly disappeared. Meanwhile, I was left to confer with the captain of the fishing boat, who was quickly adding up all the damages. By the time he was through, I am confident the United States Marine Corps wound up, paying him enough money to buy a new boat.

Thankfully, the boat trip was soon old news, and I concentrated on trying to complete active duty without any further incidents. However, there was one new assignment that was shocking.

I remember the day as I was enjoying the warm California sun and talking to a young Marine who had just returned from Nam having served with First Battalion, Ninth Marines. Assigned to the Demilitarized Zone, 1/9 was known as "Walking Death" because it took more casualties than any other unit in the war. The fact that he had made it out alive and without injury was rare. He was friendly and, like most Marines, refused to think of himself as special.

"Just doing my job, sir," was his comment to me.

At this moment, I was interrupted by a phone call from the Battalion Commander. The Colonel wants to see you immediately. This cannot be good.

"Captain, said the colonel, "President Nixon is flying into El Toro to go to his home in San Clemente, and since you are in charge of the refueler pool, I want you to refuel his plane."

I nearly passed out.

Yes, it was true, I was "in charge" of the refueler pool, but it was run by a first sergeant. I dropped in occasionally to chat but had no idea what really went on. As for refueling a plane, I did not even know how that was done.

"Don't worry," said the Colonel. "Secret Service will take care of the details. You just be certain the truck is in good working order and that security is in place."

"Yes, Sir," I said with a great deal of apprehension. I was about to get a real lesson in how much preparation goes into a President traveling into a location. A week before his arrival, secret service agents, along with all types of federal marshals, were all over the base and spending an enormous amount of time with young Captain Griswold wanting to know all about military aviation fuel (JP6) and did our records reflect compliance with proper operational procedures. I was a nervous wreck as our record keeping was hardly up to secret service standards. Our fuel was tested, and armed guards were placed around the truck. I lived in the refueler pool during this time.

The big day arrived, and as the colonel had said, the secret service and their people had taken care of the operations. I was off in the distance as the giant Air Force plane rolled into our area. The President's limousine, which had arrived days earlier, was dispatched, the President surrounded by security got in, and it quickly disappeared with all kinds of security in front and back of his limousine.

Once the President had left, it was time to refuel the plane. Air Force One is always topped off quickly after a President departs in case there is an emergency, and he must immediately fly out again. So, after the excitement of seeing the President, my truck rolled out to refuel the plane. We had gone over the truck from top to bottom, but it was an old truck. I had nightmares about what could happen. The truck would stall, or a tire would go flat, or even worse, the brakes would fail, and the truck would crash into the plane. But my worse thought was supposing one of my crackerjack troops had failed to tighten a hose coupling, and JP 6 aviation fuel would be sprayed all over the plane. A spark would ignite the fuel and Air Force One, the pride of our Nation, would be engulfed in flames. The ensuing investigation would determine that Captain Griswold was responsible.

I could just imagine the conversation back on Griswold Point.

"Did you hear that David set fire to the President's plane."

"Well, I always had my doubts."

"Oh, Lord, his poor mother."

I am quite certain a committee would be formed immediately to have my name changed. Fortunately, everything went smoothly, but the thoughts of what could have gone wrong did not allow for a comfortable time on active duty.

After the boat trip and my refueling incident, I needed a break. I had bought a brand-new Chevy convertible and threw myself into enjoying the California weather and the beautiful California beaches. I tried to put my combat experience behind me and not think too much about it. The relaxed environment of California was a big help.

Marriage

During this time, I met the girl I would marry. Patricia was her name, and she lived in a nearby town. Her family was from Alabama. They moved out to California in the fifties to find work and a more exciting lifestyle. Patricia offered an intoxicating combination of blond hair and blue eyes (that seemed to be a trend). She had the California tan combined with the southern charm and southern accent that reminded me of my mother. Our first date was a hockey game. The Los Angeles Kings were an expansion team, and they played the Boston Bruins. Being from New England, I really wanted to see the Bruins, and they were at their best. They featured Phil Esposito, Kenny Hodge, Johnny Bucyk, Teddy Green, and of course, the great Bobby Orr. The Bruins led seven to one after the first period. After one of their scores, I threw up my hands and spilled beer all over Patricia, whom I called Patty. I thought our romance was over, but she just smiled. I fell quickly and deeply in love.

After a few more dates, we spoke about marriage and began to plan a wedding. This was going to be complicated. My large family was not excited about going to California, and her family divided between California and Alabama had no intention of going to Connecticut. My sister and her family were in Texas. They were not sure what we were doing as we went back and forth, debating which coast would host the wedding. Finally, the pressure was building, and Patty was upset with all the family bickering. Out of nowhere, I came up with a brilliant Idea. We would get married in Las Vegas! There is an old saying that if you try and please everyone, you wind up pleasing no one. How true it was in this case.

"Las Vegas!" screamed my mother. "Do they even have churches there?"

My Aunt allowed she had heard of Las Vegas, and thought it was somewhere west of Pittsburgh.

"Very tacky," she added.

It was noted that no Griswold had ever been to Las Vegas much less gotten married there. Once again, I was put back on the endangered list on Griswold Point.

We were married at Chapel of the Bells in Las Vegas. It was a little building on the strip sandwiched between the large hotels of the times: the Rivera, Sands, Dunes, and Stardust. It was painted blue and white with gold trim and on the roof were bright flashing neon lights spelling out "Chapel of the Bells" A far cry from the stately New England churches of my youth.

Inside was a large room where pictures of Jesus, Mary, and the saints were replaced with Elvis, Liberace, and the "Rat Pack" of Frank Sinatra, Dean Martin, Sammy Davis, Peter Lawford, and Joey Bishop fame. There were a few chairs and an elevated platform that took the place of an altar. A piano was in the corner. The minister appeared (I guess he was a minister) and asked if we had the papers. Nevada did not require a blood test, but you did have to file paperwork at the city hall, which we had done. He glanced at the paperwork and mentioned his fee for performing the service. Cash was preferred, and I gave him the money. At that point, his rather large wife appeared and smiling at us she walked over to the piano and hammered out her rendition of *Here Comes The Bride*. The minister went through the ceremony. We said our I do's and I kissed my new bride. The large wife threw some rice on us, and we were off to Caesars Palace to see Wayne Newton.

Patty and I settled in the beautiful town of Tustin, California, just outside the El Toro Marine base. We had a lovely apartment, and soon we were expecting a baby. Life was good, and I felt blessed to have a wonderful wife, a growing family, and a steady job in the Marines. Within the year, our son was born, and my family was coming to grips that maybe things would turn out okay for the prodigal who had followed his own very different path.

Patricia Thrash Hinton
Patty

Coaching

My active military commitment ended in California, and we moved to Florida. I went into coaching and teaching. The high school was Largo High School in Largo, Florida, and the principal was a wonderful man, Gene Chizik. Mr. Chizik was a Marine, which I believe was the major reason I was hired. There is no denying the bond among Marines, and it paid off once again.

There were many dedicated professionals at the school, and I enjoyed the teaching experience. I taught physical education and one history class. But what I really liked was being a head baseball coach and an assistant on a large football staff. Mr. Chizik was a former football coach, and he was very partial to coaches. His son Gene Chizik Jr. would become the head football coach at Auburn University.

The coaches at Largo were quite a group. Springfield College took physical education very seriously, and I was prepared to follow their guidelines and teach the youngsters the finer points of games and sportsmanship. That was not exactly in the curriculum at this school. The mornings always began when the driver education teacher (another football coach) had his students leave the schoolyard and drive to the local bar known as the Gator Bar. A student would run inside and pick up for the dog racing program. The driver ed car would then make its way to the school stadium where another football coach would take the program back to the coaching office. The next activity was for a coach to call the weather station to get an accurate account of the weather forecast. With the weather information and the posting of the dogs from the program, the coaches were ready to phone in their bets at the nearby track known as Derby Lane.

Meanwhile, you might ask what was happening with their classes. Well, they had a quick way to discuss the finer points of physical education. After lining everyone up, one of the more intimidating football coaches (and they were all intimidating) would have the students count off by twos.

"All right," bellowed the defensive line coach, "ones are shirts, and twos are skins."

With that, he tossed out a football with the instructions to play. He added some further instructions.

"You piss-ants better not cause any trouble!"

With that instruction, he retired to the coach's office to discuss the racing events with other coaches and to study the offensive line play of our next opponent.

This was not exactly what I had studied in my four years of college. At first, I tried to conduct a somewhat structured program, but it was not well received. One day a message was delivered.

"Hey Springfield," growled the head football coach with a menacing glare.

"Do what you want, but if you think you are going to come down here and upset our routine, you are badly mistaken," he completed the warning by spitting tobacco juice into a coke bottle for effect.

I took the attitude when in Rome and, in time, fell in with their system. It got to be a fun time. I was the head baseball coach, and we had particularly good teams. In fact, one year, we won the Regional Championship and lost out to the ultimate State Champions by just two runs. This was quite an achievement considering we were classified as one of the largest schools in the State. In Florida, the schools were ranked by attendance, and it went from 1A to the largest, which was 5A. With over 3,500 students in grades 10 through 12, Largo has classified at the 5 A ranking.

As the head baseball coach, I was in charge, and I was totally committed to the program. I had very good and dedicated players, and I loved coaching them and the success we enjoyed. However, coaching football was different than baseball. High school football in Florida is second only to Texas in terms of intensity. All the coaches in the school participated in the football program. Along with the head coach, there were eight varsity coaches, three Junior varsity coaches, and two freshmen coaches. I was the head JV coach.

The head coach was deadly serious about winning football games for one simple reason: his job depended on winning. This was quite different than the coaches I had played under in high school and prep school in the north. Of course, those coaches wanted to win, and we were encouraged to win; but win or lose, the coach was secure in his job. Unless there was a scandal or player revolt, coaches in the northeast stayed at their jobs for as long as they wanted.

But Florida was different. First, football gate receipts covered the athletic programs. For the track team to have new hurdles or the baseball team to have new bats or the tennis team to have a good travel scheduled rested on the success of the football team to fill the stands on Friday night. All the coaches of other sports were supportive of the football program to ensure their sport was well-financed. I immediately recognized the need for football success.

Second, the entire town rallied around the football team. On Friday nights, stores closed, and restaurants were empty. Everyone was at the football game. The head football coach was an important person in the town, and winning brought recognition to a small southern town. It was good for business when the football team won.

Another factor in demanding success on the field and from the coach was the booster club. The booster club was made up of well-connected parents who held important positions in the community. The main purpose of the booster club was to provide financial supplements to the football program. High school football is incredibly expensive. The equipment alone is a big part of the sports budget. Maintenance of the field, which in Florida requires much re-sodding, water, and care coupled with the lighting of the field, was expensive. Insurance costs were daunting. Then there are all the little things. The expense of taping over two hundred ankles every day adds up. Most schools cannot support a large program without help from a booster club.

While booster clubs offer much financial assistance, there was a downside. These parents were not just writing checks for nothing. They expect a winning season.

Winning programs get recognition, and recognition brings in the scholarships from major college programs. The University of Florida, Florida State University, and the University of Miami were the three big Florida schools. Still, good programs can bring scouts and offers from Georgia, South Carolina, Clemson, Alabama, Auburn, Mississippi, and Louisiana State University. Parents of talented football players want their sons to get that exposure, and winning programs can bring results. If a coach is not winning and the program is not getting recognition from colleges, the boosters can bring tremendous pressure on a high school principal to make a change.

Finally, a successful high school football coach can be a ticket to a college job, equating to more money and more prestige. While some coaches were happy to remain at the high school level, others were driven to success as a steppingstone to the college ranks.

As a result, the head football coach demanded and received a tremendous commitment of time from his coaching staff. The two and half hours of after school practice was just the beginning. All coaches were expected to be at all the games. Wednesday afternoon for the freshmen, Thursday night for the junior varsity, and Friday night for the varsity.

Meetings were held after practice, and game films were reviewed every Sunday night.

We scouted other teams throughout the week. During football season, I was lucky to be home by ten.

While I was competitive and wanted to win as much as anyone, I thought this amount of time was unnecessary, and I clashed with the head varsity coach. Where we really disagreed on was the strategy. The head coach believed in a playbook that resembled a phone directory. All different formations, signals, and different plays for a variety of defenses and offenses. It took a great amount of study and concentration to understand and implement his strategy and system. Plus, they would change the plays and formations each week, depending on who we were playing. Even worse for the players was getting screamed at in practice for failure to run the right plays.

I strongly disagreed with this approach. The Marines had taught me KISS (Keep It Simple Stupid.) If players are confused or uncertain, they lose their aggressiveness. I wanted players who were confident in what we were doing and not concerned about what play was going to work in what situation.

Further, I recognized that high school athletes were not just football players. They had so many things going on in their lives. There was pressure to make good grades and get into a good college. That took time and study. There was money. Many came from single-parent homes where it was hard to get by financially. They had to take jobs that required work before school or late in the evenings after football practice. That led to fatigue. Others had a home life that was unsettling as parents fought, and siblings were problems. If all that wasn't enough, there were girls and the pressures of dating and all that entailed.

Recognizing the challenges faced by my players, I devised a simple system. We ran out of the I formation and only had eleven running plays and five passing plays. But we ran them every day, and everyone knew them without hesitation. As a result, we never jumped offsides, never fumbled, never made mistakes. By never beating ourselves, we wound up winning every game. Other teams knew what we would do, but they could not stop us. It also helped that I had exceptionally good players. But by keeping it simple, we were able to capitalize on our talent and win all our games.

The other factor in our going undefeated was my ability to motivate the players. Taking a leaf from my Marine training, I built my team up to believe they were the best, and no one could match us. This came to a head when after a great half time motivating speech based on *we are invincible, and no one can stop us,* my fired-up team went screaming out of the tunnel onto the field, set to destroy our opponent. Unfortunately, the band was just coming off the field, and my guys ran right through them. Horns and drums scattered, and it was a miracle no one was badly hurt. The fans thought it was great, but the band director and the principal did not share their enthusiasm.

Fortunately, we won the game, so all was forgiven.

My going undefeated drove the head coach crazy. He knew three times more about football coaching than I did, and for the JV team to win all its' games and the varsity to go just over 500 was more than he could handle. He and I did not get along, and it was unfortunate considering how successful the baseball program was and how much I liked the school.

Despite my disagreements with the head football coach, I could have stayed at Largo High School for a career. In retrospect, I was so fortunate compared to those who could not find work after leaving the military. Not only did I have the job of my dreams, but I had a supportive wife and a great relationship in the community. I had everything going for me. But underneath this Norman Rockwell existence lay memories of the Nam. They would come to life without warning.

Ira Hayes

To illustrate how the Nam could suddenly appear, I recall a trip to Jacksonville, Florida. Patty had an uncle who was stationed there in the Navy. We planned a weekend at his home. Arriving on a Saturday morning in the early spring, we enjoyed seeing Uncle Ray and his wife, Peggy. They were nice and fun. Ray and Patty talked about their many relatives, what they were up to, and I was following along.

After lunch, the three of them wanted to go shopping. I hated shopping, so I opted to remain on Ray's porch and relax. It was one of those days that makes Florida so great. Sunny and warm before the summer heat would bear down, I was basking in the sunshine, drinking a beer, and eating a ham sandwich. Ray loved country music, and the radio was set to one of his favorite stations that played the songs of Hank Williams, George Jones, Patsy Cline, and other country artists. I was enjoying the moment and looking forward to the evening when we were all going out to a well-known restaurant.

Then the announcer on the radio said the next song would be Johnny Cash singing the "Ballad of Ira Hayes." The song begins with the painful wail of Johnny's, deep baritone voice, and the drawn-out words- I R A   H A Y E S   I R A   H A Y E S. It goes on to tell the true story of Ira Hayes. Ira Hayes was a Pima Indian who joined the Marine Corps and was one of the six men who raised the flag on Iwo Jima. He survived and returned to the States as a hero to be celebrated. But in time, he was forgotten. After all, he was just an Indian, and no one really cared about him. The song ends with Ira Hayes alone and dying drunk in a ditch back on his desolate reservation.

And with that song, on this beautiful spring day, the Nam reappeared. I thought about the Indians I had served with and how proud they were to be Marines. They had so little, and the country had done so little for them, and yet they volunteered to serve at a time when many far more fortunate young men ran off to Canada. My mood darkened. I was mad at the President and his leaders for not understanding our enemy, mad at our military leaders who didn't react to enemy strategy, and was mad at the college students who protested the war. Mostly, I was mad at everyone.

Then my mood changed to the last part of the song-no one really cared. The war was winding down and would soon be over. Americans would move on. But what about the mothers, fathers, wives, girlfriends, brothers, sisters, cousins, and in some cases, the children of those who had fallen. Moving on would not be so easy for them. I had met some of them and realized just how their lives had been changed forever. And this realization was so sad and overwhelming that tears began to trickle down my cheek. The situation called for a few more beers.

Soon, Patty, Ray, and Peggy appeared. They were in high spirits and looking forward to dinner and a night on the town. I tried to appear enthused but had a hard time adjusting to the happy group.

"What's the matter with you?" asked Patty.

And this is where combat veterans have problems. How would I answer her? Telling her, I was upset because Johnny Cash sang a song would sound ridiculous. Going into detail of the loss of so many in the war would put a damper on the evening and what would they say. How could I expect them to understand how I felt? So, in answer to her question, I just said I was tired.

"Well, shape up Marine, we have a big night ahead of us," said my wife.

And I tried. We went out, and I laughed at Ray's jokes and listened to the conversations, but Nam had a hold on me. The haunting words of Ira Hayes kept going through my mind. I drank more than I ate, and by the time we returned home, I was exhausted from the weight of emotions and from more than a few drinks. Everyone sat around watching television, and I staggered off to bed.

It was around one in the morning, when I awoke. The room was spinning, and I felt awful. Not wanting to wake my wife, I got up in the dark to head for the bathroom. I planned on drinking some water and hopefully finding some aspirin in the medicine cabinet to address the pain in my head. Opening what I thought was the bathroom door turned out to be a closet door. Smashing my head on a wooden clothes hanger, I lost my balance, fell into the closet, got sick, and passed out.

My hitting the closet floor woke up my wife. She screamed.

"David, what are you doing?"

Ray and Peggy, upon hearing her scream, came into the room and surveyed the situation. Ray broke out laughing, saying later it was one of the funniest sights he had ever witnessed. Peggy was less enthused as her new shoes, along with my wife's clothes in her opened suitcase, were covered in vomit. Patty altered between embarrassment and rage. I don't remember much, but the next day I was brought up to speed on everyone's review of the scene.

I offered no excuses and just tried to shrug it off. But I felt bad for my wife and disappointed in myself for not controlling my emotions. But the memories of Nam were hard to control.

The Reserves

As part of my enlistment, I had to serve three years on active duty and three years in the reserves. The reserve unit I was assigned was in Tampa, Florida, just across the bay from where we lived. We would meet once a month on Saturday and Sunday and for two weeks in the summer. A perfect arrangement for a teacher.

The reserves were quite different than active duty. Since we only met for two days a month, there was a ton of paperwork for officers. That was followed by inspections of the troops and their equipment. The troops were different than the active-duty Marines. Most were in college, and most had good jobs. Some had great jobs. The rank structure was quite different. On active duty, the officers were at the top in terms of income, followed by the sergeants, then the corporals, and down to the privates. A private in the Marines on active duty made very little. But in the reserves, it could be reversed. A private could be working for his father or a friend of his fathers and be making more than an officer. The old sergeants who might have a modest income could have a Marine under them that he worked for on the outside. This unusual income and career status on the outside made it difficult to have the discipline of an active-duty unit. Things were a lot looser. It was an adjustment.

The training of the reserve troops was done by staff sergeants. As a result, officers spent little time with the troops. But that would change on Sunday after drill ended. I was with three other officers who had been to Nam. We all had battle ribbons on our uniforms. The troops were impressed. They looked up to us and wanted to know what it was like. Since the public, in general, offered no support and, in some cases, even contempt for us, it was nice to have a group who appeared to be interested. We were happy to oblige with war stories that grew more intense and descriptive as the beers kept coming.

The setting was a bar across the causeway from Tampa. Each Sunday after drill weekend was over, I, along with two other officers, would go to this bar and entertain the 15 to 20 troops who wanted to learn about our combat experiences. After multiple rounds, the stories got better, and the adoration grew. It was probably good therapy for us. However, it was not so good for my marriage.

It was not so much the drinking, for the most part, that was tempered by my job. I could not relate to the day to day problems that we faced. Some minor things would occur; maybe the garbage wasn't put out or something was forgotten at the grocery store, or a phone message was not copied correctly. Really small things but still upsetting for a young wife with a small boy. To me, they were nothing. I had been in combat, called in enemy fire on an enemy, saw men die, and I was supposed to be upset over this or that. I just could not relate. From her perspective, I didn't care, and, in some ways, I didn't. It was not her, she was fine, but the Nam had affected me more than I realized. It certainly was a negative factor in a marriage that was not improving with age.

To improve my marriage, advance my coaching career, and conform to my family's record of success, which was always a driving force, I needed to move into the college coaching ranks. For that, I would need a master's degree. I resigned from Largo and set my sights on graduate school. The school I selected, or rather one of the few schools that would accept me into a graduate program, was the University of South Alabama. It was located in Mobile, Alabama.

A former major league manager was the head baseball coach, and that would be good for my career. I had done very well as a high school baseball coach, and college coaching would be the next step up. After that, who knows, perhaps a professional job leading to the Major Leagues. My wife's relatives were in Alabama, and that would be a plus for her. It was a win for everyone.

But in 1974, Alabama was not Florida. Florida was a unique mixture of North and South. The east coast had a large number of citizens from the northeast, New York, in particular. The west coast where we lived had many mid-westerners, Michigan in particular. The central parts were a mixture of people from both the north and south who had less income than those on the coasts. The Panhandle was predominantly southern and was known affectionately as "The Redneck Rivera." In most cases, folks got along very well. I never felt out of place, and while all people in Florida enjoyed the Sunshine State, there was never a chant of "I'm a Floridian."

Alabama was entirely different. It was the deep south and proud of it. Montgomery, Alabama, was the capital of the confederacy during the Civil War. In the eyes of some, the war was still on. The Governor had been George Wallace, and he had made it clear that Alabama did not welcome outsiders, especially from the north. The governor was a short, stocky man who had once boxed and was often described as pugnacious. He was a die-hard segregationist and was noted for standing in the doorway of the University of Alabama and defying a federal court order to integrate the University. Even though Wallace was now out of office as a result of being shot while running for President in 1972, he was still extremely popular in the state. Many Alabama license plates had "This is Wallace Country" proudly displayed on their cars.

While the Governor cast a shadow over the State, there was another man equally popular, if not more so. He was Paul "Bear" Bryant, the head football coach at the University of Alabama. The Bear, as he was called, believed in winning football games. He would go on to become one of the winningest coaches in college football history, compiling 323 wins. From Bryant's point of view, winning with only white players was OK as long as you won. Then the unthinkable occurred, Alabama started to lose. The University of Southern California came into Tuscaloosa, the town where the university was located and beat Alabama 42-21. USC had several African American athletes on their team. Stinging from the loss, the Bear felt the time was right to recruit African Americans to Alabama. This presented folks in Alabama with an interesting choice. Hold on to segregation or win football games. Winning football games won out. Often it was said that the Bear did more for integrating the south than any politician.

While Alabama was slowly changing, it still harbored a deep resentment of northerners, and so I was a little concerned. Yet, Patty's family was from Alabama, and that eased my reservations about venturing into a vastly different part of the country. We were off to Alabama. Nam was not invited, but it followed.

When people think of military service, they immediately think of combat, casualties, and the horrors of war. No question these are present. But for me, the Nam brought about another reaction. Since I survived, there was nothing I could not do. My experiences gave me a false sense of security and an oversized ego. Two stories serve to illustrate the point.

Baseball and Raisins

Along with studying for my master's degree in education, I would become part of the baseball coaching staff at the University of South Alabama. Eddie Stanky was the head baseball coach at South Alabama. He had a long and storied career both as a player and a major league manager.

He had been with the Dodgers when Jackie Robinson broke in, and he was a staunch defender of Robinson when Robinson was harassed and threatened by the bigots of the times. He had moved on to the Giants and was there when Bobby Thomson hit the home run that was known as "The shot heard around the world." He had managed the White Sox and the Texas Rangers.

He knew lots of people in professional baseball, but his reputation varied. Given the nickname "The Brat," it was said of him, "He can't hit, can't field, and can't throw; all he can do is beat you." That was somewhat of a misstatement as he was a very good player. Still, his tremendous desire to win overshadowed his ability.

He would do anything to win, and that attitude carried over to his coaching career at South Alabama. He was a small man but large from the standpoint of controlling the situation and demanding the same from his staff and players. Nothing was more important than the execution of details that led to winning baseball games. He could be intimidating, but being a Marine, I thought I could handle him and would have no trouble coaching his players. This would be a great move for my career.

Because of his reputation and his great ability to impart knowledge to young men, Coach Stanky had recruited outstanding baseball players to South Alabama. Even though it was a small school, they won most of their games against bigger schools such as the two more well-known schools in Alabama-Auburn University and the University of Alabama. They also triumphed over all the schools in the Southeast Conference. In fact, the University of South Alabama, when I was there, was ranked seventh in the Nation. It was not unusual to have 15 to 20 professional scouts at our games. Seven of our starting players signed major league contracts that year.

Coach Stanky took baseball very seriously, and he enjoyed keeping his assistant coaches off balance. One minute, he could be extremely complimentary to efforts and results.

"Coach Griswold, you are doing a great job. I am glad you are on the staff," he would allow. Coming from a man of his experience, it made me feel great. The very next minute, he could be really upsetting.

"Where are the sunglasses for the outfielders?" he yelled at me.

I was not sure that it was my responsibility, but no matter.

"I just can't count on you!" he fumed.

I felt terrible.

His handling of players was unpredictable as well. For those who followed his instruction and gave one hundred percent, he was fine and would offer motivational messages:

"Good job! or that's the way to do it."

Coming from one who had experienced so much in baseball, the player was grateful and very motivated. But for those who were less motivated, Coach Stanky could be a terror.

I was in his office one day reviewing a game we had won without much trouble. Suddenly, he started to get upset. "Coach Griswold, get so and so in here immediately," he shouted.

We had a record of every class and where all the players were at all times. I went to a study hall to retrieve the player. Entering the room, Coach ordered him to sit down. The discussion began.

"Why didn't you go from first to third yesterday on a ball hit between right and center?" he asked.

"I didn't think," he began but was cut off immediately.

"That right, you didn't think. You haven't done any thinking since you have been here. I am not sure if you are capable of thought," said the Coach.

The player lowered his head.

"You think you can loaf around, do the bare minimum and sign a major league contract. Is that what you think?"

"No," said the player.

"Let me tell you something. There were major league scouts at that game. They watch everything you do, and not hustling is noted and recorded. Those are just the things that keep you from getting signed, and worse, it can hurt our chances of winning," lectured the Coach.

Then the player said the worst thing possible. "Well, we were way ahead," the player said in a very casual manner with a slight smile.

He was known to be somewhat of a smart-alecky. I thought Coach Stanky would pass out from rage. "You think this is funny? That we were way ahead. Let me tell you how funny it is. Do you know where I just came from?"

"No, sir."

"Well, I came from Administration, and I have put your scholarship on hold. We are paying for your tuition, housing, food, and books. That's a full ride. I have given you a full ride, and this is how you reward us?" Coach Stanky was livid.

He continued. "What do you think would happen if I pulled that scholarship? Could your family pay for your college education?"

"No, sir," said the very subdued player.

"Well, it's up to you. You can stay here and sign a contract or go back to your farm and sit on a tractor. Let me ask you, are you going to hustle on every play? Are you going to hustle at every practice? Will I ever have to have this conversation again?" Coach demanded.

"No, sir."

The coach had made his point, and the player went on to have a good year helping us win most of our games. He then signed a large contract with a professional team. His parting words to Coach Stanky were:

"Thank you for everything."

No question, Coach Stanky could be unpredictable, but he got results. He cared about his players if they produced victories, which they did. Many were intimidated by him, but I had survived Nam, so nothing affected my confidence.

As cocky as I was, I did want to fit in and be part of the program. Most of the players and all the coaches were from the deep south. Since I was from Connecticut, they were a little suspicious. I felt the need to adapt to some of their ways. One adaptation was to chew tobacco. Most everyone did, and it seemed like a good idea. The problem was chewing tobacco was terrible. The first time I tried it, I nearly threw up. I was dizzy and salivated so badly I could not talk. This was not going to work.

Then I came up with a brilliant solution. I really liked raisins, and a mouthful of raisins could resemble a mouth full of tobacco. Even better, the raisin juice looked like tobacco juice. I could load up on raisins and spit out the juice and who would know the difference. I would buy the tobacco that came in a large pouch with Red Man written on the cover, dump out the terrible tobacco, and fill up the pouch with raisins. I was one of the guys.

Players kept the tobacco pouches on the bench and would load up before the game or perhaps before going out onto the field. I was careful to be sure my "tobacco" was separate. One day there was a mix-up.

It was a Sunday doubleheader, and the stands were full with at least 15 major league scouts. We had some really good players being scouted. Television cameras were present as the game was being shown throughout the southeast. It was around the fifth inning of a close game. Coach Stanky was not happy that the game was close.

To make matters worse, our starting pitcher was running into trouble. He had given up a double to the first hitter and walked the second on four straight balls. Coach Stanky was furious.

"Coach Griswold," he yelled. "Get out there and find out what's going on with our pitcher."

This was my big moment. I would go out in front of all the fans, scouts, and cameras to impart my baseball wisdom to the struggling pitcher.

To play the role, I grabbed for my tobacco pouch of raisins and bolted out of the dugout. I was two steps out when I made a startling discovery. Someone had switched the pouches, and I had just jammed a huge amount of chewing tobacco into my mouth. By the time I reached the mound, I was dizzy and feeling nauseous. As I spoke to the pitcher, I swallowed more tobacco juice, and now I was really getting sick. The pitcher was a senior and was not too happy I was coming out to talk with him. He was joined by the catcher and the rest of the infielders. By this time, I started to weave.

"What do you think?" said the catcher with somewhat of a grin on his face.

"Uh, you need to throw strikes," I said.

"Oh, really," said the pitcher, "I never would have thought of that."

A couple of the infielders started to laugh. At this point, Coach Stanky was having a meltdown in the dugout. This was serious; two men on, no outs, and in an important game, and his infielders, along with the catcher, were grinning and laughing while his assistant coach was staggering all over the mound.

"You don't look so good, Coach," volunteered one of the infielders who would later play major league baseball for the Boston Red Sox.

"Well, lets' get two," I mumbled as I stumbled back to the dugout.

The players in the dugout had combined looks of amazement and humor, while Coach Stanky glared at me. I proceeded to spit out the tobacco and spent the rest of the inning drinking water at the cooler. By some miracle, we got out of the inning with no runs being scored, went on to win the game, and Coach Stanky calmed down. It was, however, the last time I was ever asked to go to the mound and talk with a pitcher.

The raisins were retired.

Coach Eddie Stanky

The Boat Trip

Along with my studies and coaching baseball, I spent time with my family. My wife took a job at a bank. She was smart and a very quick learner. The bank president liked her and felt she was a rising star. He was a genuinely nice and generous man. One day he asked her if we would like to take his boat out for the weekend—a nice gesture.

"David," asked Patty, "Do you know anything about boats?"

"Of course," I said. "I know everything about boats."

Keep in mind, my reference point was a 12-foot outboard with a 7 1/2 Evinrude motor, which I had as a teenager. With assurances that I knew everything about boats, my wife accepted the offer, and we were off on a weekend trip with our small son.

Entering the exclusive yacht basin, I met the boat. It was not what I expected. It was an exceptionally large Chris Craft around 30 feet. It had two powerful Chrysler inboard engines. I had never been on this type of boat, much less driven one. But again, I was a Marine, and I had survived Nam; there was nothing I could not do. Anchors Aweigh!

We unhitched the boat from its mooring, and I fired up the engines. The boat was pointed bow first out of the slip, and I gently moved the control handle forward, and the boat responded—nothing to it. We were out of the yacht basin and headed to the open seas—Mobile Bay, to be more exact. I had on a yachting hat and was practicing my wave to other boats embarked on the same journey. My little boy was enjoying all the boats, and my wife thought I knew what I was doing.

The first of many challenges occurred when I noticed that the gas gauge was near empty. That cannot be good. We would need fuel. Across the Bay, I saw a sign with a large yellow Shell emblem. I headed towards the dock to fuel up. As I pulled alongside, a dock master stood by the pumps, ready to fill up the large boat. I pulled up next to the dock and cut back on the engine. That would be fine for my 12-foot boat with the 71/2 Evinrude. However, for a 30-foot cruiser, it did not work so well. The boat kept going. The dock attendant stared in wonder as I drifted right past him.

How do you stop this thing; there were no brakes. Alarm bells started to go off for my wife. I made a large circle and gently eased the large boat towards the dock. I stopped the boat by slamming it into the dock. The dockmaster was less than pleased. He filled up the boat, and I paid him, and again we were off.

With a boat full of fuel, we motored into Mobile Bay. Of course, I had no charts, no idea of navigation, or boating rules of the road. This would be bad enough on a lake or a river, but Mobile Bay is a large shipping channel. Barges and tankers were coming into the area, and they command a wide berth. Then there were fishing boats, sailboats, and pleasure boats—a great amount of traffic on a beautifully warm weekend. I had no idea where I was heading or how to navigate in this swarm of boats and ships. To avoid one boat, I cut across the stern of a large fishing boat. Their fishing poles that were bent suddenly shot straight up. At first, I thought their waving and yelling was a friendly greeting, and I waved back. What followed was a not so friendly gesture, and I realized they were quite upset. Apparently, I had cut their fishing lines.

By now, Patty had come to the realization that I had no idea what I was doing and, in the process, had put all of us, especially our young son in danger.

"Get us out of here," was the order from the second in command.

Acknowledging she was right, I headed back to the yacht basin. By now, it was around five in the afternoon, and other boats were heading home as well. The order of return was controlled by the dockmaster. A whistle was blown, and one by one, the boats were docked.

It was now our turn. I headed into the basin and alongside our slip. The plan was to back the boat into the slip and tie up. I put the boat in reverse and headed to the slip. Unfortunately, I misjudged the dock. Realizing I was about to smash into the dock, I powered forward. That shot me across the basin and headed right towards a docked boat.

With that, I jammed it into reverse and shot back across the basin; again, headed for the dock. This was not working. A couple more back and fourths, and I was creating a small tidal wave. Boats were rocking, and the local gentry who were enjoying their afternoon drinks were less than pleased.

The dockmaster was blowing whistles, and people were screaming at me. At this point, it was obvious I could not back up the boat, so I positioned it bow first and headed into the slip.

Once again, I had no idea how to stop the boat. The momentum carried the boat into the slip and right through a beautiful white picket fence. The fence was smashed, and the boat plowed into the bank. My wife grabbed our son and fled, leaving me to offload the boat and face a truly angry mob of yachting enthusiasts, who seemed to take parking boats rather seriously.

As I stepped off the boat, I lost my balance and fell into the water. Now, I do not recommend swimming in a yacht basin. The water is dirty and churned up from the boats.

Visibility is zero. I wound up diving for items, including my car keys.

By some miracle, I found them and, waving to the horde of angry onlookers, I retreated to the car. It was a quiet ride home. The next day word had reached my wife's boss of the great boat disaster, and apparently, he was upset. Damage to the boat was minor, but the fence required repair, and he was chastised by the locals for allowing me to take out the boat. Whether my wife was fired or resigned is subject to interpretation. However, the fact that she no longer worked at the bank would be accurate.

Jobs

After the boat trip disaster, my stay at South Alabama was coming to an end. I would obtain a master's degree in education, and it was time to get a job. While my GI bill had paid for tuition, it did not cover housing, food, cars, and all the other items that any household needs. Funds were running low and more income was required. The question was, what to do next?

Again, the optimism generated by being a Marine came into play. As opposed to getting a safe job in a high school, I was ready to move on to college coaching. And not just any college. The open college job and the one I selected was at Florida State University, located at the state capital in Talahassee, Florida. Florida State had one of the best baseball programs in the country. They had beautiful facilities and a loyal fan base. It was not unusual for them to sell out a large stadium for their home games. As a result, news of the opening at Florida State brought in some high-powered coaches who wanted the job.

The head baseball coach at Florida State was a man named Woodie Woodward. Woodie was a Florida State baseball alumnus who had played in the major leagues. He had given part of his signing bonus to the university for lights on the baseball field. It was a smart move because when his major league baseball career ended, he had a good job waiting for him. I applied and was interviewed by Woodie for the baseball position.

The interview went well. We liked each other and shared many baseball stories. I offered a strong resume. First, I was a decorated Marine Corps officer. While military service at this time may have been discounted in parts of the country, it was held in high esteem in the south; Woodie was impressed. If I could manage Marines in combat, I surely could handle college boys.

Second, I had a particularly good high school record of coaching in Florida. I had taken average talent and gotten them into the regional finals. I had good contacts, and several coaches in that part of Florida would provide strong recommendations.

Third, and I believe most important, was my work at the University of South Alabama. Woodie knew Eddie Stanky and Coach Stanky had provided a particularly good recommendation. I was confident I would get the job.

The interviewing process dragged on. There were many very qualified candidates, and Woodie wanted to be fair and make sure he made the right call. As time went on, the interviewing came down to three candidates. I was one of them, and I was called back for another interview. I thought I nailed it. I was so convinced I would get the job that I never bothered interviewing with other schools. Woodie had said he would make the final decision, and I would hear back in a week or two. Patty and I would be off to Tallahassee, and I started to look at houses in the area.

The letter came in the mail with Florida State University in bright red letters on the envelope. I opened it up, expecting to see the word Congratulations at the top. Instead, it started with *Thank you for applying for the position of baseball coach at Florida State University*. I did not need to read any further.

The selection for the position was a baseball coach named Mike Martin. I felt I had more leadership qualifications, but he had one thing I had not really thought of during the interview. Mike had been in Florida high school baseball coaching for a long time and was continually active in baseball associations throughout the state. He would be able to recruit the best high school athletes, and as most know, recruiting is a key in major programs. Further, he was a Florida State alumnus who had worked in the past with Woodie, which I did not know.

As it turned out, Mike Martin was an excellent choice. He served as head baseball coach at Florida State University for forty years. During that time, he won 2,029 baseball games, a record in Division I college baseball. I doubt I would have matched that record.

No question, Woodie made the right decision.

For me, it was a serious setback. The interviewing process had taken us to the end of the summer, and all the good coaching jobs were filled. Now, what would I do?

I made it clear that California was out. Partly based on the California lifestyle, which I did not like but mostly because I had no contacts. No one could help me get a teaching/coaching job. My family's contacts were from Boston to Washington. They had no influence in the south or midwest, and west of the Mississippi was foreign territory. Many in the Griswold family felt the west was still controlled by cowboys and Indians. It is safe to say my family was far more familiar with London and Paris than any city in the West.

Patty's family would reach out, but their contacts were in the trades. The thought of me working in construction, automotive, or manufacturing was laughable. To this day, I cannot fix or repair anything.

The high school jobs in the south were all filled, and my contacts were limited. That left New England. Here my family could help. Between colleges and prep schools, I could obtain interviews, and even at this late date, be hired at least as an assistant coach. Even more important, I had a fallback. If nothing worked out, I could get employment in my old hometown, and there was free housing on the family compound. My mother and all my relatives were very supportive of my return. Going back to New England was the smart move; and the safe one.

With that in mind, I left Patty and our son in Alabama and journeyed north to secure work or at least secure a place to stay. From my perspective, things were going to work out.

But for my wife, a pending move to New England was as bad a choice for her as California was for me. First, she was a southern girl who had grown up in the warm weather of Alabama. Her family had moved to the sunny beaches of California, and she liked the beaches. The cold New England winters were a big negative for her.

Second, her immediate family was in California, and her other relatives remained in the south. But no one on either side of the family had ever ventured north of the Mason Dixon line. She would be 3,000 miles away for her immediate family, and 1,500 miles away for her other relatives.

Third, and maybe most important, was her feeling that my relatives had not fully accepted her. That may not have been true as most were positive, but there were a few who had been cool and could be snobby at times. I recall one time at a cocktail party when one family member who had graduated from Vassar asked Patty what college she had gone to.

Expecting to hear one of the seven sister schools, Patty said Rio Hondo College, which was a small junior college near where they lived in Whittier, California. Patty was an excellent student, but her family had limited income and was not able to send her to the better-known schools. When informed that the college was Rio Hondo, my distant cousin remarked:

"Rio Hondo, why that sounds like a car."

It was a funny line, but it was also insensitive and cruel. I am not sure Patty heard it, but I did, and I was really angry. It was one side of my family that could be irritating. This idea that because they had money and the contacts to get into the most prestigious schools, they could look down at others. As mad as I was by the comment, I was willing to let it pass. But to a young wife from another part of the country, this attitude was upsetting and concerning.

As time went on, I was being pulled to New England by my family, and Patty was pulled to California by hers. Compromising in Kansas was not discussed.

It should therefore not come as a great surprise that while I was looking for work in New England and staying at my mother's home, the phone rang. It was Patty. I jumped right in with a quick rundown of job possibilities. There was a long pause on the other end.

"David, I want a divorce." I was caught short and had little to say.

"I will come down to Alabama, and we will talk about this," I replied. That ended the phone conversation.

I flew down, and it was clear the decision had been made. We met the lawyers, and it was over quickly.

For the first time in my life, I had no answers or no will to fight. The thought of my son going to California was devastating, and yet it was the right move. Patty was a devoted mother, and our son was only five. I had no reason to contest that decision. The lawyers droned on, and I just sat there and agreed to everything. I took my clothes, some family silver, a few pictures, and one of my most prized possessions, which were my Boston Red Sox beer mugs, and drove back to Connecticut. It was the longest and worst drive of my life.

Returning to Connecticut, the divorce was a major setback. No one in our family got divorced. It just didn't happen. Once again, I had fallen short. To make matters worse, the divorce was expensive, and now I was returning home with no wife, no job, and no money. This would not be well received. My mother was very sympathetic and offered love and encouragement. But the rest of the family was extremely disappointed, especially with the no money part. Both my uncles had been generous in helping us get started in our marriage, and I had let them down. I was 32 years old, and at a time when most Griswold's were moving ahead in their careers and positioning themselves for a prosperous income, I was out of work and broke.

My mother had remarried and lived in a large house with her new husband. The house had an apartment attached to it, and I moved in. Her husband was a wonderful man, and his support was very meaningful to me. His name was John McCook.

John was the middle son of three boys and on his way to a highly successful law practice in New York City. A graduate of Trinity College in Hartford, Connecticut, John had gone on to receive a law degree from Harvard University where he graduated Magna cum Laude.

He was very smart, and his quiet, thoughtful demeanor made him extremely efficient in overseeing legal issues.

John came from a very distinguished family. His father was Judge Philip McCook, who had been a colonel in the Army serving in the Judge Advocate General's office to the Army during World War II. Judge McCook was awarded the

Legion of Merit for his service. Later, he became a well-respected judge in New York City. Judge McCook would gain prominence as the Judge selected to preside over the trial of the most notorious criminal of the times, Charles "Lucky" Luciano. Luciano had organized the five crime families of New York who would put a vise grip on American business throughout the country.

The prosecutor in the Luciano trial was a young lawyer named Thomas Dewey. This was the same Thomas Dewey, who ran for President in 1948.

Thomas Dewey and Judge McCook had Luciano sentenced to deportation back to Italy. As a result of deporting the most feared gangster in the country, the McCook family had grown up with guards around their New York home as they feared retaliation from the Mob.

During this time, Thomas Dewey and John McCook became good friends, and it was rumored that if Thomas Dewey had been elected President, John McCook would be his choice for Attorney General of the United States. Sadly, for John, Thomas Dewey was defeated by Harry Truman in one of the greatest upsets in poitical history.

Shortly after that, John left New York and moved to Connecticut, where he established a small law practice in our town.

Despite his education, family background, and success as a New York lawyer, John's life was marred by tragedy. His older brother had died in the war, and his younger brother was killed in a car accident. His first wife had died prematurely from cancer, and if that wasn't enough human misery for any one person, his oldest daughter, a beautiful young woman of 22, was killed in a car accident coming home after her senior year in college.

Most men would have been bitter if not hateful for all this loss. But John was not. He served as a senior warden in the local church, and I never met anyone who lived a more Christian life.

As smart as he was, I believe John saw through my kidding around and realized the war combined with the failure of my marriage was taking more of a toll on me than I was ready to acknowledge or accept. Perhaps it was because his father and brother had served in the military coupled with all the pain he suffered that he could in some way, relate to my state of mind. He was always encouraging me to succeed and never made me feel ashamed for having to move into his home. In short, he was one of the kindest, most generous men I have ever met, and he helped me to get my life back on track.

But again, I was haunted by living at home and being dependent to some degree on his generosity.

**My Stepfather
John S. McCook**

Realizing I needed income, I got a job as an assistant baseball coach at Yale University. The job came about through a combination of family connections and coaching contacts. I had met the head coach at Yale when they played South Alabama on a spring trip.

"Well," said my uncle, "He couldn't get a degree from Yale, but I guess he can be a coach," spoken with a limited amount of enthusiasm.

I was grateful to have the opportunity, but coaching baseball at Yale was vastly different from South Alabama. Coach Stanky at South Alabama had been intense, and the players were there to someday play professional baseball. At Yale, the players were going to be engineers, lawyers, doctors, businessmen, and government officials. Playing baseball was fun, but let's not get carried away. No one was going to sign a major league contract.

The best part of Yale baseball was the head coach, Ken McKenzie. Ken had pitched for Yale and was unusually good for the Ivy League. He was one of a very few from the Ivy League who had ever signed a professional contract and wound up on the original Mets, considered by most to be the worst team ever assembled. His stories of that first year with the Mets were hilarious.

Recognizing that the players at Yale were a far cry from the majors, Ken would spin tales to the players and fail to get overly upset at the outcome of games. One of his favorite stories was the first time as a rookie he faced the great Hank Aaron, one of the greatest hitters in the history of the game. Ken struck him out on a slider, and after the game, he approached the great hitter and asked him to autograph the ball. Arron tended to be aloof and not happy to be struck out by a rookie. He grabbed the ball, instantly signed it, and tossed it back to Ken without saying a word.

About a month later, Ken was again facing Aaron and "Hammering Hank" as he was known, hit a mammoth home run far over the left-field fence. As he rounded third on his way home, Aaron yelled out to Ken,

"Hey rookie, if you find that ball, I will sign it too."

I really enjoyed Ken while coaching at Yale.

The Painting Company

Coaching baseball was fun, but I needed to make more money, so I formed a painting company. We would paint local Connecticut houses, many of which were large colonials that would need painting every five or six years. There was plenty of work, and I was excited to be an entrepreneur. Operating my own business would be well received by my family. After all, they owned businesses. Granted, my business was small, and painting houses was a far cry from Wall Street, medicine, or engineering, but it was a start. I thought I would finally get on track with family expectations.

I had assembled an interesting crew of two Vietnam Veterans, one college student, two local high school kids, and an older fellow who was kind of the foreman. There is a common belief that painters like to drink, and this crew did its best to live up that stereotype. Truthfully, they did good work, and I should have made significant money. However, there were distractions.

One time my older foreman who was badly hungover, fell off a ladder into some lady's prize peonies. The women loved those flowers, and they had won ribbons at the local fair. Not that year as the peonies were ruined, and I had to pay for their restoration.

Another time, my painters managed to spill gallons of paint on a beautiful hardwood floor, and that was an expensive cleanup. It all started on a Friday after lunch when my crew was painting a beautiful old colonial home dating back to the early 1700s. They were using oil paint as that was preferred on older buildings of historical significance. I stopped by to motivate the crew.

"Guys, you are doing great work. Here is a case of beer to enjoy over the weekend. I will be back at five to give you your paychecks."

"Thanks, boss," sung out the foreman. Everyone was quite happy, and I was basking in the adoration of being a great business owner with a dedicated and highly motivated group of employees.

When I returned at five, the scene was rather chaotic. It seems the fellows had decided to drink the entire case of weekend beer. I should add it was about 95 degrees, and they were painting inside with no air conditioning.

One painter had passed out inside a closet and was being attended to by another genius who was pouring beer on him to revive his buddy. Another had gotten sick and thrown up on the front lawn, which was not a pleasant sight.

But worst of all was the paint that had been spilled all over beautiful old walnut stained floors. The floor had to be sanded and stained at my cost, and that took care of the profits for that job.

Another time we had a big job painting the local shopping center. There was ivy on the back walls, and as we prepared to paint the woodwork by cutting off the ivy, one of my painters sliced through all the phone lines. That knocked out all the phones in the complex, which was not too well received by the business owners. That was also an expensive repair. Then, there was the time my team lost control of a ladder and managed to drop it through a large plate glass window. I never realized how expensive large windows are to replace.

But by far, the biggest loss was when my highly trained team got the address wrong and began scraping the paint off the wrong house. It was an honest mistake. I had written the address down in a hurry, and my "foreman" glanced at the paper. Twelve Hillside Lane. The painters arrived at eight in the morning, but I had some supplies to pick up, so I didn't arrive until ten. When I got to the job, there were no painters to be found. Where were they? I can't believe they didn't show up. I continued down the lane and around a corner where, to my surprise, there were my painters fast at work at Seventeen Hillside Lane. In two hours, they had done a super job of taking the paint off the wrong house.

I called out to my foreman, "What the hell are you doing?"

"Taking the loose paint off. Should be ready to paint by this afternoon," came his enthusiastic reply.

"It's the wrong house."

"What? I have it written here-17 Hillside Lane."

"That's a two, not a seven," I said.

"Looks like a seven to me," emphasized my foreman.

As we were discussing the difference between a seven and a two, one of the town's finest police officers appeared. He was a friend of mine, sort of. We had grown up together and played on the same baseball team. But I was the better player, and I felt he was a little resentful of that fact. Now the tables were turned. He was in a power position, and I was a mere house painter.

"We got a call from a very upset homeowner," he said with a slight smile across his face.

"There was a mistake," I volunteered

"You think so?" the officer said, this time with an even wider smile.

"I will speak with the owner and clear it up," I said.

"Allow me to help," said the officer who was really enjoying the moment.

Inside the house, we met the owner, a little lady around seventy who was terribly upset over her home being invaded by a gang of painters.

"I am terribly sorry about the misunderstanding, but your house could use a coat of paint, and I am prepared to give you a very good price," I said. I was hoping to get a job and even a small profit out of this situation.

"Well," said the lady. "I never have had my house painted by someone else. My dear husband always did the painting, but he died a few years ago in a fishing accident."

"She is a poor widow," said the officer just to help with the negotiations.

"I am so sorry," I said.

"Yes," the widow continued, "He was a commercial fisherman and got caught in the nets," she hesitated, and her eyes were filling up.

Any hopes for a profit were gone, and now I was merely trying to cut my losses.

"Well, we will paint the house for free and simply charge for the paint," I volunteered.

"Under the circumstances, you being a Griswold and all, I think you should throw in the paint for free," said my old baseball friend.

"I guess we could do that," calculating in my head what this was going to cost me in supplies and labor.

"Thank you so much," said the window who seemed to have quickly recovered from her tearful memory of the departed fisherman.

To placate the police, avoid a lawsuit, and keep my business license, I had to paint her house for free. Of course, the story of painting the wrong house spread quickly in the town. For my successful family having a family member

owning a painting company that was becoming the laughingstock of the community was not going over too well.
It was time for a career change.

Career Consulting

I moved on to career consulting and worked in New York City. A Marine hired me for that job. His name was Earl Bark, and he resembled Earnest Hemmingway in looks and spirit. Earl had served in combat in Korea and was open to taking chances. He took one with me. I knew nothing about how to consult on a career-I was looking for one myself. Earl said I would do well because I had majored in education and, most of all, because I was a Marine. I had serious doubts. After all, New York City was the capital of international business, and I would be asked to help those who know a great more about the business world than I did. To say the least, I had reservations. Realizing he had some selling to do to convince me, Earl and his Vice President, Harold Gallagher, invited me to a business meeting.

The meeting took place at the New York Playboy club in a private room. Along with Earl and Harold, there were three beautiful Playboy bunnies. They were serving us drinks and bending over in the process to show off some amazing assets. I was greatly impressed. I was also on my way to getting slightly drunk. As time passed, and Earl and Harold kept telling me the virtues of helping people find jobs, the drinks kept coming. I hardly heard what they were saying as I concentrated on looking at the bunnies. Soon I found myself saying yes, I would work for them in New York. So, someone who had no idea of corporate business began as a career consultant in one of the largest consulting firms of its kind in the country.

My family was shocked.

"David on Madison Avenue in New York, I can't believe it," said one of my cousins.

"Well, he will never make it," said another.

But to all their amazement, I did well. It was a wonderful experience, and my prior adventures were most helpful.

While I had been challenged in academics, especially in math and science, consulting played to my strength. I could write resumes and could simplify problems resulting in solutions. But by far, my greatest strength was my ability to relate to the clients.

If they were well educated and upper class, I would toss in my Yale connections. If they were hands-on and came up the hard way, I would relate Marine Corps experiences. If they loved sports, I would talk about my baseball experiences.

If by chance, we did not connect, I would just reassign them to another consultant. It was a perfect place for my skill sets, and I really did well. Even better, I was surrounded by other consultants who could help me out when I was confused.

But the real key was Harold Gallagher. Harold had a Doctorate degree in Behavioral Science from the University of Pennsylvania. He was extremely smart, combined with great insights into people, and why they acted or responded to certain situations. I was fascinated by his abilities, and he apparently saw something in me. We became friends, and he was a mentor to my development as a career consultant. With Harold's help and Earl's support, I became the leading consultant in the New York Office. I could have stayed there for the rest of my career.

While I enjoyed the service side of the business, Earl felt it would be good for me to understand sales in the aggressive world of New York City. Sales was a vastly different world from my military experiences. It involved a completely different set of skill sets. The salesmen and women were all on another floor, and it was an education to watch them in action. Two stood out as being the best.

One was Tim. Tim came from some money, but his money was nothing compared to his wife's. Lauren was a part of one of the most prosperous families in America, dating back to the '20s, when elite families controlled most major businesses.

They owned four homes, including a large apartment in New York, a monstrous old house on the water in Rhode Island, a beautiful villa on the inland waterway in Florida, and a farm in Pennsylvania. Each house had staff that managed the property along with the boats and cars.

I had never seen such wealth.

My family would be considered well off, but no one in our family had this kind of money. Tim and his wife introduced me to a world that I did not know existed. Going out with them in New York City was exciting. I do not think they knew the subway existed. Cabs were taken unless it was a special evening, in which case a limousine was ordered.

One of their favorite spots was a private club on Central Park South. At the club, everyone knew everyone, and Tim was very gracious to introduce me to people I had only read about in the papers. The dinners were feasts with all sorts of appetizers, salads, entrees, and decadent desserts.

Waiters fell over each other to be sure our water and champagne glasses were never less than half full. The conversation was always pleasant, and talk centered around where they would spend their next vacation. With four houses to choose from, it was a challenging decision.

What really amazed me was their total lack of concern for the politics of the day. They had so much money that it did not matter what the government did or who was in charge.

They had teams of accountants and financial planners to protect their assets. It was a different world. That came home to me in another setting.

I had walked into Tim's office one day, and in a friendly way, Tim said. "David, that suit is terrible. You need some new ones."

"I guess so," I said, somewhat embarrassed.

"Thanks, where do we go?" I asked.

"We do not go anywhere," said Tim with a smile.

Tim picked up the phone and made a call. About fifteen minutes later, a tailor entered the office and presented Tim with a book of color splotches.

"Well," said Tim, "This one would look good, and this one, and let's see I think this one."

I agreed as Tim had excellent taste.

The tailor took my measurements and disappeared.

A couple of weeks later, Tim called me and said, come on down to his office.

I entered, and there were three beautiful wool suits, all custom made to fit me perfectly. I thanked Tim and asked him how much I owed him, figuring it would be a month's paycheck.

"Don't worry, you're a good friend," Tim said.

With that, Tim signed a slip of paper, and it was done. And that was the fascinating thing. Tim never paid cash, wrote a check, or pulled out a credit card. Everything from clothes to dinners to gifts was signed for. The bills would be sent to one of their banks and paid by someone Tim probably did not even know. I was impressed.

As for his job, which was to sell career services, Tim had an approach that could only be duplicated by one who did not need money. That was not typical. Most salesmen always need money because they tend to spend it as fast as they make it. But in Tim's case, that was not a problem. In fact, one time over a few drinks, Tim volunteered that there was no way they could spend all their money. Their multiple investments brought in way more than the family spent-and the family spent a lot.

Tim would meet a prospective client in his very beautifully decorated office, wearing one of his many custom designed suits with a very conservative Brooks Brothers tie and wing-tipped shoes, and offer the prospect coffee or tea from a Tiffany cup and saucer. Very classy.

Tim's sales approach was to spend as little time as possible, talking about the service. What he did talk about were trips, cars, houses, paintings, private clubs, material things. All intended to impress and subtly suggest that whatever wealth the prospect had could be greatly enhanced with our service. Tim was so confident, so smooth, so proper, and so charming that it was an easy sale presentation. Anyone would enjoy the conversation.

The close was always in the first meeting, known as a one-step. After an hour of name dropping and discussions of social status, Tim was ready to present the price for our service. This is the critical moment in sales, and Tim delivered in a manner that was very matter of fact.

"So, Bill" or whoever he was speaking with at that time, "Here is the price for our service," and he would push a piece of paper in front of Bill.

If Bill nodded, the sale was concluded, and Tim would celebrate with a snifter of cognac or brandy.

If Bill hesitated or stated it was a lot of money, Tim would be shocked. This was not faked. It was real. The amount of money was what Tim and his wife would spend on a casual weekend party. Tim's response was to stare at the person in disbelief, but he never would say anything.

"Wait for them to say something," he told me later.

Often the person would be so embarrassed, they reluctantly would agree to the terms. If not, Tim just shook his head and dismissed the prospect as being a waste of time. Tim would never dwell on a lost sale. The person was not worthy, and Tim would pour himself a drink just to ease the pain of having to have spent time with such a lost soul. He was one of the best salesmen simply because he never pushed. He never had to.

After my learning experience with Tim, Earl said I should meet Sal. Sal was a native New Yorker and worked his way up from a humble background. He was hungry and extremely aggressive. Sal had to make money because he had a large family that lived in a small house in Queens. His family depended on his sales success. Sal's sale approach was a little different.

"Have a seat. Any trouble finding us?" Sal asked with absolutely no interest in the answer. "Let's get started."

Sal launched into what is known as the probe. He would ask question after question regarding the prospect's career. If the person was happy or pleased with a certain area, Sal quickly skipped over it. If the person expressed disappointment or frustration, Sal pounced. He told me later it was like a dentist probing your teeth. He had to find the cavity, the soft spot. Then inflict as much pain as possible to make the prospective client realize they needed help.

For example, Sal would ask about money.

"Well, I was well paid in my past job," said the prospect.

Since that was not the answer Sal was looking for, he immediately asked another question.

"What are you looking to do next?"

"I'm really not sure," the prospect volunteered

"Not sure," Sal was almost screaming. "You have to be sure. How can you succeed if you have no idea where you are going?"

The prospect appeared rattled and said he might consider it.

Sal interrupted him, "Might consider, what kind of an answer is that? Might consider! You will never get anywhere with that approach. You need our help. Tell you what I am going to do because I really care about your situation," said Sal.

"I'm going to consult with our staff and see what we can do. When is your schedule clear?"

The prospect paused and gave a date.

"Good," said Sal." Now I want you to get here on that date, and you must bring your wife with you. We need her understanding and support."

What Sal wanted was to be sure the man would not say he needed to discuss the fee with his wife and leave. Scheduling a second meeting was known as the two-step close.

I was entirely uncomfortable with this approach, but to my amazement, the prospect agreed.

"Come in next week," Sal told him

The next meeting was truly painful.

First, Sal described the prospect to his wife as a floundering person with little hope of success on his own. Then he proceeded to question the wife to determine her role in the decision making process. That was critical.

When it came time to present the price for the services, Sal told the couple the service was needed to save his career, his family, and his marriage. Sal told them the amount and then said he would leave the room and let them talk it over. Sal and I exited, and he smoked a cigarette and told me this was the moment that separated the men from the boys.

"Watch me, but do not say a word," Sal instructed.

I said, "Of course."

Sal entered the room with a cheerful "What do you think?"

"Well," said the prospect, "I like the program, but it is a lot of money."

"What?" said a very serious Sal." A lot of money? Let me ask you a question. How much did you pay for your last car?"

Before the prospect could answer, Sal continued, "and what is it worth today? It went down in value-right?"

"Yes," said the man, and his wife had to agree.

"Well, our service will only increase in value. This is the best investment you can make."

"We need some more time to think it over," said the prospect.

"What is there to think over? You know you need it. It must be the price? Is that it?" Sal seemed angrier and angrier, which was well-rehearsed.

At this point, I felt so bad for the couple I was ready to pay for their service myself.

But Sal was relentless.

"Tell you what I'll do. I will break the fee into a monthly payment plan. I am not supposed to do this, but I think management will approve. How's that?"

Normally that would work, but in this case, the wife said in a very sad tone.

"It is just too much."

Now Sal was mad, and it was not faked. He was mad. "You mean to tell me after all this time together, you are not willing to invest in our service to improve your career. I can't believe it. Just leave."

With that, Sal got up, opened the door, and the couple walked out looking forlorn and feeling terrible.

I think I felt worse.

After they left, Sal showed why he was so good. Instead of second-guessing himself or his techniques, he simply said,

"I have got two more today, I will get them for sure."

Never did he doubt his strategy.

In speaking with Earl later, I remarked on how different the two sales approaches were. Then Earl told me something that was the secret to his business success. He said:

"David, the real key is Karen, the administrator. She is the one who assigns the prospects to the salesmen. Both Tim and Sal are successful if they are matched with the right prospect. But they are disasters with the wrong prospects. Always put people together who share things in common."

It was great advice and has certainly helped me in my business career. I genuinely enjoyed my time in New York, and Earl and Harold were wonderful teachers who helped me to excel in a career that I enjoy to this day. Yet, I found myself missing my son, who had moved with his mother back to Alabama from California. I thought If I lived in Atlanta, I would be able to see him on the weekends. It was time to move.

Earl Bark

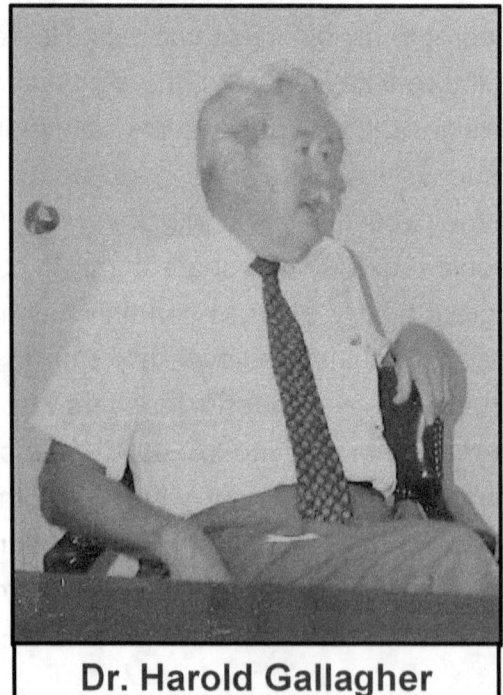
Dr. Harold Gallagher

After three years in New York, I bid farewell to my friends and headed to Atlanta, Georgia. I did not know anyone, but the company had an office in Atlanta, so I had a job. The Atlanta office was not as challenging as the one in New York. That allowed me more time to spend with my son. It was a good decision.

I found the business world in Atlanta to be vastly different than New York. New York was fast-paced. Time was money, and you needed to respond quickly to get ahead. The business was everything, and people were driven to succeed.

Atlanta offered a different style. Business was important, but it could not be rushed. You took your time, and social graces were expected. A business meeting required some pleasant introductions and discussions of current topics in a congenial manner. Being pushy and aggressive was just not acceptable. Once pleasantries were over, you got down to business but in measured tones and always politely. After the fast pace of Manhattan, I enjoyed the change.

The success of the Atlanta office revolved around two saleswomen-Christian and Tamara. Christian came from New Orleans, and the rumor was she had been a Madam in the French Quarter on Bourbon Street. I cannot verify that, but she did look the part. Christian dressed in tailored clothes that were designed to accent her dynamic figure. While her outfits were expensive, they were just short enough or tight enough to have a "come hither" effect. She accented these outfits with strings of pearls, bracelets, and rings. Her hair was long, curled, and very blond. Her makeup was well done but just heavy enough to catch your attention. Men could be mesmerized by her looks, and she played that to her advantage.

Christian's sales approach was to greet her client and always find something to compliment. Flattery went a long way with men, especially in the south. After the compliments, Christian brushed over our services. She spent time inquiring as to what the man had accomplished and how he was on the verge of something big. It was a fortune-teller type of presentation. *I see great things in your future*. With our help, you can achieve a wonderful new life. All this was done with a warm smile and a voice that dripped sincerity. It was amazingly effective.

Tamara was not quite as dazzling as Christian but made up for it by being even more complimentary. She had been born and raised in Atlanta and knew how to charm southern men. Basically, she agreed with anything they said and endorsed whatever they wanted. If the prospective client said they wanted to be Chairman of Coca-Cola, Tamara would insist that was possible. If the prospect wanted to double his income, well, of course. If the prospect wanted to build a business from scratch, no problem. Just sign here. Tamara's other hook was name dropping. She knew or said she knew everyone in the city. Introductions to the movers and shakers would happen quickly, once they were a client. That, too, was an amazingly effective approach.

While these techniques got the prospective clients enthused and interested, the key was in the close, asking for the money. This is where Christian and Tamara excelled. In New York, Sal always wanted the wife in the second meeting to keep the prospect from saying he had to speak with the wife. Christian and Tamara would never allow a wife to be present. They both knew a wife would see through the charm and flash and kill any deal. They had a well-rehearsed plan if the subject of *I must speak with my wife* came up.

"Really, you want to speak with your wife?" they would say. "I am surprised. You impressed me as a man who made a decision for himself," they would offer with a sweet smile. If that did not work, they would continue.

"Now I am a woman," pausing to let that obvious statement resonate with the prospect; "And I know what women want." The prospect was all ears.

"Women," they would continue, "Want to be surprised by the success. When you walk into your home and announce you have obtained a new career that will bring more income and prestige to her life, she will be impressed and very, very happy. Believe me, I know." Although not said, the batting of eyes and raised eyebrow accompanied by the most seductive smile, indicated the wife would be sexually forthcoming. This close brought results, and Christian and Tamara led the Atlanta office in sales. Sales for the Atlanta office was not a problem.

The problem was in the delivery of services. Unlike New York, where they were many high paying jobs that made for successful clients, Atlanta was a much smaller market. There were not as many high paying jobs to meet client expectations. Many of the consultants were not as well trained as those in New York, and sometimes the Atlanta clients fell short of their goals. Worse, Christian's charms were absent once a sale was made, and Tamara's promises of knowing everyone in Atlanta never seemed to materialize. As a result, there were a lot of unhappy clients, and that led to refunds. While Christian and Tamara were among the sales leaders in the company, they were at the top of the charts in client refunds.

My enjoyment of the business culture in the south was offset by the complaints from Christian and Tamara's sales.

These complaints, based on a lack of client success, led to refunds, and I was the one who had to deal with refunds, which were never pleasant. Frustrated, I wanted more from business and felt I had enough experience to take the next step.

A consulting firm out of Boston offered an opportunity to open a branch office in Atlanta. I flew to Boston and agreed to put up money to open an Atlanta Branch. This was a big step. Working for someone is one thing. Making an investment with your own money is quite another. There are big risks if things do not go well.

I set out to hire and train a group of consultants to operate the office. I was extremely fortunate to find two men who would lead the initiative and become good friends. Ron Jones was a soft-spoken consultant from Mississippi. He was very smart, and his southern ways fit perfectly into meeting the needs and expectations of our clientele. He was a great sounding board for me, always encouraged me, and gave me the support I needed. We have done business together for over 35 years, and his ability to focus clients and supply research has led to thousands of success stories. The lead salesmen was Don, a hard-charging Army colonel from New Jersey. His drive and ability to sell were perfect for the sales side of the business. With these two men leading the way, our office became very successful.

I was happy with the results and learned aspects of the business from a new perspective. One piece of my education was my relationship with the Boston owner. In addition to my salary, I had agreed to a percentage of profits from the office. In retrospect, I should have taken a percentage of the office gross. I quickly learned there was a big difference. The gross is what is taken in, and that is quite easy to calculate. While the percentage would be lower, the money to me would have been greater, and there would not have been any arguments.

On the other hand, the profits or net was what was left after all expenses and taxes were subtracted. I got an education into how nets can be manipulated. One big area was the nebulous term of corporate overhead. Corporate overhead represented the assistance our Atlanta office would receive from the headquarters in Boston. All the accounts payable and receivable, payroll, and office expenses would be paid from Boston. I had no problem paying our share of these expenses. But other expenses, including administrative charges for trips, meetings, and office conversations, were initiated by the owner and his wife. Those charges were subject to many discussions and differing points of view.

My conversation with the owner regarding charges usually went as follows:

"Hi, Dave, what is going on? How can I help you?" said the owner in an overly friendly manner.

"Well, I am not sure about the latest report. It seems more expenses were taken out than I expected."

"Dave, Dave, let the accountants worry about that. You just concentrate on the great job you are doing. By the way, how about those Red Sox."

He knew I liked baseball and was a master at changing the conversation.

These types of conversations went on monthly, and it was nearly impossible to get him to address my concerns. The major concern is that I was being taken. The funny thing was, I liked him away from the office. He was very smart and had a masterful way of negotiating to his advantage. I respected his talent, but at the same time, I wanted to be treated fairly. It was an uneasy relationship, and it never improved over time.

Elaine

During this time in Atlanta, I met my wife of over 35 years. Her name is Elaine, and she came into my life at the right time. She has dark hair and brown eyes. I felt it was time for a change from blond and blue eyes.

We met at a church singles event. Having failed in my attempts to find the right partner in most of the bars in Atlanta, I had gone to this church event to find the right person and to partake in a very inexpensive meal. As I was in the dinner line, the server gave me the last piece of lasagna. As I put it on my plate, a voice from a lovely girl behind me said, "Thanks a lot."

"Well," was my snappy comeback, "You will get the fresh stuff." She just smiled in a friendly manner.

As we moved down the line, I was in the process of trying to avoid a woman who wanted me to join a bible study class. As I saw her approach out of the corner of my eye, I turned around and asked the winner of the fresh lasagna if I could join her. She smiled again and said yes. We sat down, and the conversation just flowed. There was no pressure or concern, just an easy discussion of our lives. As it turned out, she too was divorced.

While my marriage had come apart from location concerns and family pressures, Elaine's had failed as a result of having little in common.

They had married in their hometown of Syracuse, New York, and had moved to Atlanta for his employment and from Elaine's perspective to escape the cold. He was a teacher by trade yet took a job as a butcher in Atlanta, where he spent most of his days in a meat locker.

Elaine had obtained a certification in respiratory therapy and had a good job at Georgia Baptist Hospital. I had always been partial to women who worked in the medical field.

In college, most of my dates were at a nearby medical school. In the following years, I had dated many nurses, therapists, and administrators from hospitals and doctor's offices. I liked them because they were compassionate and giving, which drew them to the field. Also, they were practical, having to deal with the serious reality that not everyone came home from the hospital. Unlike models and fashion designers who could have a meltdown over the slightest provocation, medical professionals were realists, and I liked that in people. Even better, they had a strong appreciation of healthy male bodies. From my view, that was a trifecta.

As Elaine told me, their two careers were a strange pairing. Elaine spent her days in a warm, nurturing environment where everyone worked hard to bring comfort, medications, and care to the afflicted. While she was in the hospital saving lives, her husband spent his days with a meat cleaver, chopping up dead animals. As she reflected, they really did not have much to discuss at the dinner table; but on a brighter note, they did eat well.

The major concern in their marriage was children. Elaine wanted children, and her husband had failed to deliver. Perhaps it was spending his days in the freezing meat locker. I always thought that would be a great topic for a convention of urologists.

Divorce was inevitable. Elaine ventured to the singles dinner at the church to find someone who shared her interests.

Our first date was to an Atlanta Braves baseball game. We hit it off and fell in love.

We were married a year later, and she has been a true blessing, and she seems to understand me as well as can be expected. Along with her kindness and love for people, her practical and somewhat cautious approach to life is a perfect balance to my optimistic and sometimes impulsive decision-making style. With respect for each other and an acknowledgment on my part that some measured approaches to life would be a healthy change, we have made a happy life together.

I made good on my pledge to provide children, and we were blessed with a wonderful boy. Thirteen months later, we completed our family with a beautiful baby girl. Our two children are now grown and doing very well. In all, I have two boys and a girl, a daughter and son in law, and five grandchildren. I am so proud of all of them.

As a result of my tenuous relationship with the Boston owner, I would leave Atlanta. I had been there for twenty-two years and found it to be an exciting and vibrant city. But I missed New England and my many friends. So, when our children graduated from high school, Elaine and I moved back to my hometown. In many ways, I had come full circle back to where it all began.

Elaine B. Griswold

My Children:
Jeffrey D. Griswold, Eric D. Griswold, and Laura Griswold Wentz

Conclusion

Reflections

It's been quite a journey from the 1940s to the present. I have been privileged to meet many wonderful people along the way. From New England to the Mid Atlantic to Florida, I have traveled up and down the east coast and always enjoy the trip as well as the times I spent in those states. Also, I have enjoyed living in the deep south and appreciate their love of this country and perhaps a simpler way of life. One state, in particular, is Louisiana (Yes, I am a Saints fan). Their love of music, sports, and good times are unique to the country. I love and respect the solid folks of the mid-west, the proud people of Texas, and the beautiful western states. Another unique state is California, which is, in many ways, is so different and yet in others so American. In all the states with all their differences, it is the people that make us the country we are. And that is the secret of America. Despite our faults and missteps, it is the people that make this country so great.

Their commitment to hard work, their love of family, their respect for our country, and their generosity to others in times of trouble make them standout throughout the world. I have enjoyed knowing so many of them and sharing some wonderful times.

As for the Vietnam war itself and the training and deployment we endured, it fades in and out of memory. I keep in touch with the Bear and Kel, and we get together from time to time. We talk about families, sports, politics, and business. If we discuss the Marines, it usually involves the funny stories of basic training. SSgt Vic and the many things he would yell at someone. But the Nam is seldom discussed. It's hard to discuss. We did not lose-at least while we were there, but we didn't win either. And talking about those who didn't make it back is painful, and I think all of us to some degree are left with survivor's guilt. We survived, and they did not. It's best not to think about it.

Further, we find ourselves trapped between a political misjudgment on what could have been a victory and those who feel we never should have been there in the first place. The debate over the military strategies were so divided between a cautious approach and those who wanted a more aggressive one. We were the ones who were in the field fighting a determined enemy without the full support of our leadership; it is painful and hard to discuss.

Another painful factor is the perception that everyone who served in Vietnam was acting improperly. That perception was foisted on the American people by Hollywood. Look at the three movies that came out in the late '70s and early '80s: "Deerhunter," "Apocalypse Now," and "Platoon." These movies had big-name actors and were well done from a cinematography perspective. They were box office smashes that made a lot of money for the industry. "Platoon" was recognized as Best Picture of the Year. But look at the messages.

In the Deer Hunter, released in 1978, Robert DeNiro stars, and the story centers around three young men from blue-collar backgrounds who go off to war. It is well done, and the actors are first-rate. But the story deteriorates into soldiers shooting heroin and playing Russian roulette.

In "Apocalypse Now," released in 1979 starring Marlon Brando and Martin Sheen, we have an Army colonel gone mad, and an Army captain is sent into the jungles to assassinate him. We are also treated to Robert Duvall, arranging a surfing party in the middle of a firefight.

In "Platoon," Charlie Sheen narrates the tension between two sergeants played by Tom Berenger and William Defoe. Well played by the actors, it did have some realism in that there was tension between the old guard (lifers) and the younger soldiers (short timers). But one sergeant shooting the other one took a rather strong turn from reality.

Now I was in a Battalion of approximately 700 Marines. If you count constant rotation of personnel, I will say I met around 1,200 Marines. Add in my years before and after Vietnam, and that number would triple to around 3,500. Then add in all the service members I have spoken or met over the years to include my business along with the VFW and American Legion, and the number could reach nearly 6,000. My point is no one has ever spoken or confirmed or even implied anything that resembles colonels gone mad, shooting heroin, playing Russian roulette, or surfing in a firefight. But that was Hollywood's anti-military message to the American people.

As a result, one can hardly blame the American people for the perception that all who served in Vietnam were crazy. The military had lost total control, and troops were all on drugs, shooting each other, and killing the poor innocent Vietnamese Now, I will acknowledge that in the '70s, after I left, morale was poor as our role was to pull out. Those left behind were not motivated to be the last ones killed in a war that was not going to be won. With over 2.5 million serving in the war, some bad things did occur. But it was such a small percentage, and to characterize all of us in these roles is just totally unfair and not at all accurate.

I have had people ask me about my drug use and how many innocent unprovoked killings I committed. They seemed shocked when I say to my knowledge none of that happened, and it hurts as I remember all my troops and how hard they fought, how dedicated and disciplined they were, and how they did their very best under very difficult circumstances.

Upon further reflection, I find a combination of amusement and annoyance at politicians, football coaches, and the public in general. They make comments such as when you're at war with the other team or at war with business competitors or from a political discussion-we should immediately go to war against the other side.

I can guarantee you none of them have ever been to war. For us who were in war, there is no comparison; it's horrible. The loss of life at such a young age, the decision that one must make that effects the lives of others, and the enormous cost in resources are difficult to even calculate.

Further, the long-term effects of combat are even harder to calculate. Others experienced more combat than I did, but I still wake up screaming at night if the dreams take me back to those times, and that was fifty years ago. War should always be the last resort. On the other hand, to reduce the military and defense expenditures or say we should never use force does not strengthen us but, in my opinion, weakens us. It can encourage aggression. Thus, there is a balance required between having the force and using force. It takes a skilled leader to navigate that process.

I joined the local Veterans of Foreign Wars (VFW), and they made me the Commander. Great bunch of guys. Many served World War II and Korea as well as Vietnam. The older ones never complained. They did their duty with honor and came home to raise families and support their country and community. A few examples of their service stand out.

One man, Charlie Gellatly, lied about his age and entered the Navy at fifteen. He drove a landing craft on the shores of Iwo Jima and made it off the beaches.

"The greatest fear was getting the craft hung up on the coral rocks. If that happened, you were a sitting target for their large guns," he told me.

He had a great sense of humor and was always smiling. Happy to have survived and always willing to help other veterans.

Another one, Ed Wolcott, flew twenty-six missions in a B-27 over Germany. Shot down on the twenty-seventh, he spent two years recovering in a hospital. Went on to fly for commercial airlines. He told me, "The reason I survived was the cold. It was literally freezing at the altitudes we were flying, and my bleeding was cauterized by the cold. I was lucky."

Their comments were typical of all who served in those times. They were glad to have served and proud of what they did. But it was talked about with humility, respect, and with a little humor thrown in. They truly represent the Greatest Generation, and I respect them all.

In the VFW, we have several programs that support the community, and often we would go into the schools for Veterans Day. It is always a proud moment for us. The school puts on a program for the Veterans, and it is nice to be recognized for our service. I have been asked to speak on these occasions, and this is my speech.

> Thank you for the opportunity to speak today.
> When people ask me, what did you gain from military service, my first thought is the very different people I served within the Marines. They were all good guys, and we became

friends during basic training. The first person I met in our training platoon was Steve, an outstanding football player from California. Steve was 6'4" and over 200. His best friend was John from Long Island; 5'9" and maybe 160. Then a coal miner from West Virginia; tough guy. A farmer from North Dakota; easy going. A rancher from Montana; big and strong; an Indian from Oklahoma; tremendous physical shape; a Texan from the Beaumont area; funny guy, a soft-spoken southern gentleman from Virginia, a battle-hardened former enlisted man from Arizona, a baseball player from Ohio, and the Harvard graduate that I mentioned earlier. They were all different, and I went into detail on the differences. But despite the differences, they all came together. And my point was that is what makes America so great. That people from all backgrounds, creeds, and races can come together as one. In this case, they all came together to share one thing in common. They were United States Marines. They also shared another thing. All of them have their names on the wall in Washington. They gave their lives, so we could enjoy ours, and I thank all of you today for remembering them and all who sacrificed for our freedom."

That ended my speech, and it was well-received. It was nice to see the students show appreciation for the sacrifices that others have made for our country. I was proud to have been asked to contribute.

As the years pass and as I grow older, I am blessed to have the opportunity to reflect on so many adventures. I was extremely fortunate to have the coaching experiences in the south and at Yale and Trinity. The opportunity to run a business and the great consulting experiences both in New York City and Atlanta, Georgia. I learned so much from so many and truly enjoyed the experiences. I recall the early days of Coach Kehoe, Coach Mahken, and Coach Stanky in baseball. I remember those who gave me a chance; Mr. Heyniger at Darrow, Mr. Chizik at Largo High School, and Earl Bark along with Dr. Harold Gallagher at the consulting firm in New York City.

Then there were my family relatives, especially my two uncles. It is hard to say exactly how they influenced me. But I think their high standards and faint praise drove me to excel. Of course, my parents were there. My Dad, who died when I was young and my great desire to make him proud. I wish he had been present at times when I did achieve. I like to think somewhere in the great beyond he was watching. Then my mother, who was committed to my education and so supportive when times were hard. I was truly blessed to have such wonderful parents. My lovely wife, children, and grandchildren are in a special category and are so important to me. I am fortunate to have a wonderful relationship with all of them.

But of all the people and adventures I experienced, there is no question my service in the Nam had the greatest emotional impact.

It gave me the confidence to persevere. My attitude is I survived Nam; I can survive anything. Any business success I have enjoyed is far more from perseverance and being surrounded by good people than by any brilliant strategies on my part.

Along with confidence, the Nam evoked another attitude. It has given me an appreciation for the things in life we so often take for granted. I appreciate the creature comforts of a warm fire in the winter and an air-conditioned building in the summer. A delicious meal enjoyed with good friends and the thrill of a sporting event when your team wins. I appreciate the easy way in which we can move around the states and the world. I am grateful for the ability to obtain the work of our choice and change jobs if we so desire. But perhaps most of all, I appreciate the freedom to live our lives without fear. Those things were not present in the Nam, and it made an impression on me.

Today, I live in my old hometown and assist military veterans in finding jobs. With the help of many excellent and very well qualified people, we have helped thousands improve their careers. I feel it is my small way of giving back for having been spared in the Nam.

As I sit at my desk each day and try to help veterans, I have many pictures on my wall. But the two that stand out are right in front of me. One is a picture of the Marines I went through training with, and the other is a list of all those who died. There are over forty on that list and why they are there, and I am here is something I cannot answer. I am so lucky and grateful for the life I have been granted.

Looking back, I have held many titles since I left college: Captain, Teacher, Coach, Director, Senior Consultant, and Commander to Managing Partner, and even Company President. I am eternally grateful to so many whose skill, teaching, patience, and support have allowed me to obtain those positions. But in the end, when it is all said and done, there is only one title that has special meaning for me. Let me be remembered as a United States Marine.

David H.W. Griswold was born into a very successful family who owned the Griswold Manufacturing Company in Erie, Pennsylvania. Relocated back to the family compound in Connecticut, David attended public schools before going off to preparatory school.

David graduated from Springfield College and later obtained a master's degree from the University of South Alabama. He enlisted in the United States Marine Corps where he attained the rank of Captain. He served a year in Vietnam as a Company Commander and was decorated for his leadership in combat.

David went on to teaching and coaching football and baseball at Yale University, Trinity College, the University of South Alabama, and Largo High School in Florida before entering the consulting field in New York City.

David held management roles for several consulting firms before starting his own consulting business which he has continued to this day. As a consultant, David writes marketing materials to promote his clients, and his company has been recognized for helping over 4,000 men and women to achieve career success. He has authored numerous articles and been published in a variety of journals and publications.

This is his first book.

www.ingramcontent.com/pod-product-compliance
Lightning Source LLC
Chambersburg PA
CBHW071220080526
44587CB00013BA/1441